3/06

Louis Pasteur

Louis Pasteur

REVOLUTIONARY SCIENTIST

ALLISON LASSIEUR

FRANKLIN WATTS
A Division of Scholastic Inc.
New York Toronto London Auckland Sydney
Mexico City New Delhi Hong Kong
Danbury, Connecticut

Photographs © 2005: Art Resource, NY: 54 (Image Select), 9 (Erich Lessing/Heeresgeschichtliches Museum, Vienna, Austria), 97 (Snark), 80 (Snark/Musee Pasteur, Paris, France); Bridgeman Art Library International Ltd., London/New York: 31 (Baron Antoine Jean Gros/Musee Toulouse-Lautrec, Albi, France, Lauros/Giraudon), 50 (Antoine Laurent de Lavoisier/Musee National des Techniques, Paris, France, Lauros/Giraudon), 56 (Sebastien Le Clerc/Bibliotheque Nationale, Paris, France, Lauros/Giraudon), cover (Private Collection), 53, 113 (Private Collection, Archives Charmet); Corbis Images: 33 (M. Angelo), 6 (Bernard Annebicque), 13, 61 (Bernard Annebicque/Sygma), 110 (Archivo Iconografico, S.A.), 73 (Anthony Bannister/Gallo Images), 28, 90 (Bettmann), 86 (Ron Boardman/Frank Lane Picture Agency), 98 (CDC/PHIL), 83 (Owen Franken), 66 (Historical Picture Archive), 40, 103 (Hulton-Deutsch Collection), 18 (Mingasson de Martinazeau/Archivo Iconografico, S.A.), 64 (Charles O'Rear), 17, 43 (Gianni Dagli Orti), 75 (Keren Su), 20 (Adam Woolfitt); Getty Images: 26 left (Lee Boltin/Time Life Pictures), 8, 44, 78, 89, 92 (Hulton Archive), back cover ghost, cover background (Three Lions/Hulton Archive), 2, 14, 26 right, 36, 116 (Time Life Pictures), 94, 119 (Roger Viollet); Mary Evans Picture Library: 60 (R. Cooper), 47 (Becquet Freres), 77 (Jahandier), 63 (G. Piotti-Pirola), 24 (Smeeton Tilly), 35, 65, 68, 100, 104; North Wind Picture Archives: 84; Superstock, Inc./Walter Seaton: 109.

Library of Congress Cataloging-in-Publication Data
Lassieur, Allison.
 Louis Pasteur : revolutionary scientist / by Allison Lassieur.— 1st ed.
   p. cm. — (Great life stories)
 Includes bibliographical references and index.
 ISBN 0-531-16753-4
 1. Pasteur, Louis, 1822–1895—Juvenile literature. 2. Scientists—France—Biography—Juvenile literature.
3. Microbiologists—France—Biography—Juvenile literature. I. Title. II. Series.
 Q143.P2L26 2005
 509'.2—dc22   2004030449

Contents

This beautiful landscape is located in the town of Arbois, France. The Pasteur family moved to Arbois in 1827.

CHAPTER ONE

Early Life

The small, medieval village of Dole, France, sits in some of the most beautiful landscape in the country. Today, it still looks like it did on December 27, 1822, when a young military veteran, Jean-Joseph Pasteur, waited anxiously for word about the birth of his second child. Soon it came. He had a son! Jean-Joseph and his wife, Jeanne, were overjoyed. They named their baby Louis. Their daughter, Virginie, was very happy to have a little brother.

HUMBLE TANNERS

The boy who would become one of the world's most celebrated scientists was born into a hardworking but ordinary family. Louis's great grandfather Claude and his grandfather Jean Henri had both been tanners. A tanner is a craftsperson who prepares leather hides. Jean Henri and his wife, Gabrielle, had a son, Jean-Joseph, in 1791. Jean-Joseph would one day become Louis Pasteur's father.

Soon tragedy came to the Pasteur family. Jean-Joseph's mother, Gabrielle, died about a year after her son was born. Jean Henri later remarried, but he died only a few years later. Jean-Joseph was sent to live with his aunts in the French town of Salins. Young Jean-Joseph became an apprentice to a local tanner.

THE PASTEURS AND THE NAPOLEONIC WARS

World events would eventually change Jean-Joseph's life. In 1796, when Jean-Joseph was only five years old, the French commander Napoléon Bonaparte took control of the French army. Eventually he became the emperor of France. Napoléon's goal was to conquer all of Europe. By 1811, war was still raging throughout Europe. That year Jean-Joseph was

A workman tans a hide for the leather industry. Leather is animal skin that is chemically modified to produce a strong, flexible material that resists decay.

conscripted, or drafted, into the French army. Jean-Joseph was a very good soldier, and in 1812, he was promoted to the rank of corporal. A year later he received another promotion.

Jean-Joseph's greatest military success came in 1814 at the battle of Bar-sur Aube, when the French army was outnumbered five to one. Jean-Joseph's battalion fought with so much courage that it later earned the nickname "bravest of the brave." Later, Napoléon himself gave special awards to Jean-Joseph and his fellow soldiers. In 1814, Jean-Joseph was promoted again, this time to sergeant-major. By this time Jean-Joseph was a loyal and passionate believer in Napoléon and everything he hoped to accomplish for France.

When the French military eventually lost the war in 1815, Napoléon was exiled to a distant island, Elba, and France once again became ruled by monarchs, or kings. Jean-Joseph was angry and disappointed. He saw Napoléon's defeat and the restoration of the monarchy as a bitter personal disgrace. He would remain a loyal Napoleonic soldier for the rest of his life.

Some saw Napoléon as a tyrant, while others praised his efforts toward democracy. He was ultimately defeated because he tried to please both the democracy and the oppression.

The Napoleonic Wars

One of the greatest and bloodiest periods in European history occurred between about 1789 and 1815. Two conflicts were fought during this time. The first one was the French Revolution. The unrest and violence that came from the revolution caused the second conflict, which became known as the Napoleonic wars.

In 1789, the French people had grown angry and discontent with the French monarchy. The people revolted, starting the French Revolution. The French kings and queens, along with members of many other noble families, were overthrown and killed. The country was then ruled by a series of nonroyal leaders who fought for control. The violence and fear brought on by the French Revolution turned other European countries against France. Fighting between France and other countries broke out all over Europe.

In 1796, a brilliant French military commander named Napoléon Bonaparte took control of the French army. He quickly conquered Italy and Austria. In 1799, Napoléon returned to France and named himself emperor. His goal was to conquer Europe. By the time Jean-Joseph joined the army in 1811, France had become the most powerful country in Europe. Napoléon was getting close to achieving his goal.

In 1812, Napoleon invaded Russia. In Russia, his army collapsed because of the cold temperature, disease, and starvation. By then many other European countries, including Great Britain, Russia, Prussia, Spain, Portugal, Austria, and Sweden, had allied together to defeat Napoléon. On March 31, 1814, Napoléon surrendered in Paris. He was exiled to the island of Elba in the Mediterranean Sea. In 1815, he returned to France and marched to Paris with a new army. He was defeated in the Battle of Waterloo in 1815 and was once again exiled, but this time to another island, St. Helena, in the South Atlantic. Napoléon died there in 1821.

JEAN-JOSEPH STARTS A FAMILY

After the wars were over, Jean-Joseph returned to his profession as a tanner and settled in Salins, France. One day, while washing his leather hides in a nearby river, he spied a young girl on the opposite shore. Her name was Jeanne Roqui. Jean-Joseph was smitten with the bright-eyed beauty. Jean-Joseph and Jeanne were married on August 27, 1816. The new couple soon moved to the nearby town of Dole, where their first son, Jean-Denis, was born a few weeks later. Sadly, he died after only a few months. Two years later daughter Virginie was born, and Louis arrived four years after her. Louis and Virginie had two younger sisters as well. Josephine was born in 1825, and Emile arrived in 1826.

The Pasteurs lived in a modest stone house near the banks of the canals of Dole, along with other tanners who used the swift water in the preparation of their leather hides. Jean-Joseph spent his days behind the house, turning hides into leather for shoes and other items. Jeanne kept house and took care of the children. The tanning business did not make the family rich, but they were comfortable.

GROWING UP IN ARBOIS

In 1827, Jean-Joseph had a chance to acquire a tannery in the nearby town of Arbois. He no longer had to use his backyard for his business. There was an opportunity for the business to grow. The tannery also included a living space for the family upstairs. So when Louis was five years old, Jean-Joseph moved his family to Arbois.

Louis and his sisters grew up living above their father's tannery.

Louis could look out the windows of his house and see the rushing Cuisance River flowing and acres of vineyards on the slopes beyond. He and his friends swam in the river, fished, and played the usual childhood games, including catch, capture the flag, and marbles. In the winter, the children skated on the frozen river and sledded on the snow-covered vineyard hills. The best time of year was the fall, during the grape harvest. Arbois was famous for its wines, and the entire town helped in the harvest. There were feasts and games for the children of the town, and Louis took part in it all.

It was in this beautiful part of France that Louis experienced the security of a loving family and a tight-knit community. From his father, he learned the value of hard work and dedication to a craft. His mother taught him devotion and a sense of family.

Louis Pasteur Birthplace Museum

The small house in which Louis was born still stands in the French town of Dole. It is located along the bank of the canal where Louis's father started his tanning business in the backyard. Today, Pasteur's first home has been turned into a museum. The museum includes three sections. One is a reproduction of the inside rooms, decorated and furnished as they probably were when Pasteur lived there. Another section of the museum is a reproduction of a tannery workshop much like the one Jean-Joseph might have had. The third section includes an exhibition about Pasteur's scientific work and how it has affected modern science.

YOUNG LOUIS STARTS SCHOOL

Louis started first grade in 1831. Classes were held in one room of the town hall. Louis's first teacher was a young man named Mr. Renaud. Renaud made a lasting impression on young Louis, giving him a respect for learning that would last throughout his life. Much later, after Louis had become a world-famous scientist, he would fondly recall his first teacher and the lessons he learned in the small, one-room school.

Louis was an average student. In class Renaud taught by dividing the students into groups, allowing one student to teach the rest. It was a great honor to be chosen as a "monitor" of a group. Louis was sometimes chosen, but nothing in his early school days suggested that Louis would become a great scientist.

This replica of a sitting room is in the Louis Pasteur Birthplace Museum.

During long walks, Louis and his father had discussions about his future. His father wanted him to become a teacher.

CHAPTER TWO

School Life for Louis

Jean-Joseph had great plans for the future of his only son. Louis would someday become a teacher at the local university, the College d'Arbois. At the time, having a teaching career was an impressive ambition for the son of a lowly tanner. If Louis stayed in school and became a teacher, he would be the pride of his family.

Jean-Joseph took it upon himself to give Louis lessons. On many weekends, the father and son took long walks through the beautiful region. Jean-Joseph told Louis tales of his military adventures, and the two of them had long discussions. Louis's father was still very loyal to France and to the ideals for which Napoléon once fought. These experiences and his father's stories instilled in Louis a great love of France.

FAMILY FRIENDS INFLUENCE YOUNG LOUIS

One of Jean-Joseph's good friends was Bousson de Mariet, an intelligent and lively professor at the College d'Arbois. He visited the Pasteur home often, telling Louis wonderful tales of brave and heroic Frenchmen from the past, as well as stories about recent events. Mariet eventually became Louis's unofficial tutor, giving him informal lessons at home. By the time Louis was in secondary school, he had become an excellent student, winning several academic prizes.

Another family friend who spent time with Louis was Mr. Romanet, the principal of the College d'Arbois. He challenged Louis to think for himself and encouraged his enthusiasm for learning. Louis thrived under all this attention, and Romanet watched as Louis went from an average student to a young man full of excitement and dedication to learning, especially science.

LOUIS GETS AN EXCITING CHANCE

One day Romanet approached Jean-Joseph and Louis with an idea. He suggested that Louis, only fifteen years old and still in secondary school, was smart enough to get into the École Normale Supérieure, one of the most prestigious universities in Paris. Only the best students in France went to the École Normale Supérieure. Graduates of the École were guaranteed the most elite and prestigious teaching positions in the country. To get into the university, however, Romanet was convinced that Louis would have to go to secondary school in Paris.

Louis wasn't sure he wanted to move so far from home. Jean-Joseph, too, was uneasy. Why should his son go to school in Paris when there were perfectly good schools in the neighboring town of Besançon? Louis didn't need to go to the École Normale Supérieure. Besides, Paris was too expensive. How would a young boy live alone in a huge, strange city?

The answers came from another family friend, Captain Barbier. Barbier worked in Paris as a municipal guard, but he was originally from Arbois and spent many vacations in his hometown. He assured Jean-Joseph that he would keep an eye on Louis. He also told him about a secondary school in Paris that was run by Mr. Barbet, a gentleman from the area who would give the Pasteurs a discount on the fees. Also, Louis's school friend Jules Vercel had already decided to go to Barbet's preparatory school. Louis would not be alone in the city. Jean-Joseph and Louis agreed to try. On a bleak, rainy day in October 1838, Louis and Jules boarded a coach for Paris.

Louis's education began in a one-room school, but led him to study in the huge city of Paris.

DISASTER IN PARIS

Before the coach even arrived in the huge city, Louis was overwhelmed by homesickness. It was the first time he had ever been away from his family. He was surrounded by strangers, only one in a crowd of boys living in dormitories and eating together in one large hall.

Louis's grief did not go away. Even the rigors of study couldn't take

Louis was extremely homesick even before he arrived in Paris. He was relieved when his father took him back to Dole.

Louis's mind off his misery. He even confided in Jules that if he could only smell the tannery, he would feel a lot better. But the familiar smells of home were far away. Even the master of the school, Barbet, tried to cheer up Louis. Nothing worked.

Only a few weeks later in mid-November, Louis was told that someone was waiting to see him. It was his father. Jean-Joseph had come to take his son home.

Louis was certainly relieved to be going home. But he also felt a keen sense of failure. Though it would take a long time for Louis to recover emotionally from this disaster, he learned many lessons from the experience.

A LOVE OF ART

Once Louis got back to Arbois, he returned to his local secondary school and turned his attentions to drawing and painting. During his childhood, he had become quite a good artist. His teachers had encouraged him. Now he focused on art as a way to rebuild his confidence, which had been badly shaken by his terrible experience in Paris.

Louis began sketching and drawing his family and friends. He was careful to record the tiniest details in his art. He was obsessed with observing his subjects and getting everything right about how they looked, even down to the frowns on their faces. The people of the town took him seriously as an artist. He drew anyone who asked, which eventually included most of the important people of Arbois. Louis even drew the mayor's portrait. People began to think that Louis should become a professional artist rather than a teacher.

Louis's Portraits of His Parents

While Louis was living at home he drew portraits of his parents. The drawing of his mother shows a calm woman in a cheerful bonnet tied with a bright bow. She looks out of the picture with a straightforward gaze. Louis's father, Jean-Joseph, also looks out of his portrait with steady, clear eyes. He is dressed in a formal, severe suit, which was popular in the day.

Jean-Joseph was unhappy with Louis's potential career choice. Art was only a distraction, he insisted. Even the failure in Paris did not deter Jean-Joseph's ambition for Louis to become a teacher. Louis seemed to agree.

By the end of Louis's final year in secondary school, he had won several academic prizes. Some of his confidence had returned. To Louis, the idea of attending college did not seem as frightening as it had in Paris, especially if he could attend a school closer to home. Romanet urged Louis to continue his studies. Louis began to think he might be able to attend the École Normale Supérieure after all.

There was no way he would return to Paris yet. Instead, it was decided that he would go to the royal college of Franche-Comté in Besançon. Besançon was the capital of the region, and Jean-Joseph often traveled there to sell his tanned hides. It seemed the perfect place for Louis to take another try at living away from his family.

Louis decided to study philosophy and art. When he wasn't studying, he was drawing. He drew his fellow classmates, teachers, and important people in the town. In August 1840, when he was eighteen years old, Louis received his bachelor of letters degree with only average grades. It wasn't good enough for him to gain acceptance into the École Normale Supérieure. To be accepted into the École Normale, Louis needed a degree in science. Louis returned to Besançon for a second year to earn a diploma in science.

Pasteur went to college in the city of Besançon, France (above). It is the capital of the province of Franch-Comté.

It was during this year that Louis began to form the study habits and develop the focus that he would carry with him throughout his life. He spent a great deal of time studying mathematics and science. He also was offered a job as a substitute teacher, which he gratefully accepted. This position gave him room and board and a small salary. Between his studies and his work as a teacher, Louis became a happy and excited student.

ANOTHER DEFEAT, ANOTHER AMBITION

In August 1841, Louis took the exam to earn his degree in science. He and his family were confident of his success. Louis was cocky and felt that the exam would be very easy, but it wasn't. Louis failed the exam. He was devastated. If he wanted to attend the university, he had to spend another year at Besançon.

This was a terrible blow to Louis and his family. In many ways, it was worse than his failure in Paris, because then he was only fifteen years old and able to return to his family. This time he was almost nineteen and on his own. Even his family began to doubt that Louis was smart enough to make it, but, determined to succeed and humbled by his failures, Louis returned to school once again.

This time Louis buckled down. He put his art aside and focused on his schoolwork. He got up early and went to bed late. He soon rose to the highest ranks in his class. This hard work paid off in the summer of 1842, when Louis passed the exams for his degree in mathematical sciences. But there was still one hurdle to overcome: He had to pass the entrance exam to the École Normale Supérieure.

LOUIS FACES A DIFFICULT TEST

The entrance exam was given in two parts. If students passed the first section, they were eligible to take the second. Louis passed the first part, however, he found out that he had not scored very well. Dissatisfied with his poor score, Louis made an extraordinary decision. He chose not to take the second exam, even though he had qualified for it. He decided to spend another year preparing for the entrance exam. By this time, Louis had become much more confident of his abilities. He wanted to be the best. For him, it was the only choice he could make.

Even more surprising, Louis decided to move to Paris to prepare. He was apprehensive, but he knew that he was older and more certain of himself. He also knew that the only way that he could become a good scientist was to study with the best scientists and teachers in France, and the only place to do that was in Paris. He would face the city once again, but this time he was determined to succeed.

Louis went back to Barbet's preparatory school that he had left so disgracefully a few years earlier. He spent all his time studying or tutoring students to earn extra money. He rarely socialized with the other students or explored the delights of Paris. He was consumed with his science, physics, and philosophy classes. Even on his afternoons off he chose to debate and discuss scientific topics rather than relax. Louis had learned the lessons of his defeats well. He would not make the same mistakes again.

All of his efforts paid off. In 1843, he won several science awards, which boosted his confidence. He also retook the entrance exam to the École Normale Supérieure, this time ranking fourth in his class. Louis was going to attend the university.

Pasteur moved to Paris at the age of twenty-one to attend the prestigious École Normale Supérieure.

CHAPTER THREE

Cracking the Mystery of Crystals

Louis Pasteur entered the École Normale Supérieure in 1843, when he was twenty-one years old. He had left the timid, home-sick boy of his past far behind. The Pasteur who began school in October of that year was a mature and confident young man.

THE ÉCOLE NORMALE SUPÉRIEURE AND SCIENTIFIC STUDY

This prestigious school was founded in 1794 as an institution specifically focused on training professors, scholars, and intellectuals. It attracted respected French scientists and scholars as professors. Several well-known scientists of the day, including mathematician Antoine-Augustin Cournot and astronomer Victor Puisieux, were among the professors at the university. This caliber of teaching drew the brightest students from throughout France. By the time Pasteur became a student, the university was known as one of the best universities in the country.

Until the end of the 1700s, scientific research was considered to be a hobby usually pursued by wealthy aristocrats. "Science" as a branch of study or as a profession was unheard of, but around the time the university was created, science was beginning to earn a new respect throughout the world. People began to realize that science could be used to understand and to better humanity. A new interest in other sciences, including chemistry and biology, created a great deal of excitement throughout France.

Improvements to the manufacture of glass lenses in the early 1800s made microscopes much better instruments for science. It seemed possible that science could unlock the answers to almost any problem that people faced in the world.

British scientist, Robert Hooke, drew this illustration of a fly's eye (far left).

Near left, is an example of one of Robert Hooke's compound microscopes.

A Marvelous Invention

No one is sure who invented the first microscope. However, one of the earliest microscopes was created by a Dutchman named Zacharias Janssen in the late 1500s. He combined several glass lenses in a long tube to create a crude compound microscope with weak magnification.

The man historians call "the father of microscopy" was Antoni van Leeuwenhoek of Holland. He lived from 1632 to 1723. He increased the magnification of the microscope by experimenting with different types of lenses. Leeuwenhoek became a world-renowned and respected expert on microscopy.

An Englishman named Robert Hooke was also experimenting with microscopes during this time. He was the first to see and describe cells when he looked at a sliver of cork through a microscope. He examined hundreds of other objects, including tiny animals, plants, and snowflakes. In 1665, he published a book titled *Micrographia,* which described his observations.

PASTEUR FINDS HIS PASSION

It was in this atmosphere of excitement that Pasteur plunged into his studies at the École Normale Supérieure. Although he had been interested in science for several years, there was something about the university that switched on a light for Pasteur. He became passionate about science. The wonder of research and experimentation and the thrill of discovery took hold of him.

Jean-Baptiste Dumas, a French chemist, was a pioneer in organic chemistry and analysis.

The teachers at the university fueled some of this passion. One of the most influential was Jean-Baptiste Dumas. Dumas was considered one of the greatest teachers at the university. He had begun his career as a chemist and pharmacist, and through his studies of the human body became one of the founders of organic chemistry. When Dumas lectured, all eight hundred seats of the amphitheater would be filled. Pasteur would always be sitting in the front. Pasteur became fascinated with chemistry and its applications.

Pasteur was devoted to his studies with a single-mindedness that began to alarm his friends and family. He rarely socialized with his fellow students, preferring to spend all his free time working, experimenting, or studying. Sunday afternoons found him in Dumas's laboratory, taking private lessons from the lab assistant there.

Pasteur spent his three years at the university so absorbed in his work that he barely noticed anything other than science. His ambition had now outrun his father's humble wish for his son to teach at the local college. In the presence of great scientists and thinkers and competing against the brightest students in France, Pasteur began to have loftier dreams. He was good enough to be a teacher at a larger university, perhaps somewhere in Paris, perhaps at the university itself. And maybe, just maybe, he would be good enough to become a great scientist in his own right.

MORE TESTS, MORE DISAPPOINTMENTS

At the end of Pasteur's three years at the university, he faced another important examination. All students took a competitive test, called an *agrégation,* when they completed their studies. After that they would get an appointment as a teacher. The French government, along with scientists and other educators, assigned teachers to positions all over France. Teachers were given assignments based on their experience and on their field of study.

Hooke's Famous Flea

Robert Hooke's book *Micrographia,* published in 1665, is famous for its amazing illustrations of the tiny organisms he saw through his microscope. One of the most famous is an image of a flea, which Hooke drew himself. The original drawing is 18 inches (46 centimeters) across. Another famous drawing shows a head louse gripping a strand of hair. That illustration is almost 2 feet (61 cm) across.

Pasteur passed the agrégation easily. When the results were announced, Pasteur had ranked third in the physics part of the test. His examiners showered him with praise, saying that among all the new graduates, Pasteur was the only one who knew how to teach.

Pasteur, expecting a good assignment, left Paris to spend the holiday with his family in Arbois. He was there when the news of his appointment finally came. He was to become the professor of physics at the college of Tournon, a small, insignificant school in the French countryside. Both Louis and Jean-Joseph Pasteur were bitterly disappointed.

Pasteur did not want to accept this post, so he immediately hatched a plan. He wrote to his famous professor, Jean-Baptiste Dumas, asking for a teaching position at the newly created École Central in Paris. Dumas did not respond to Pasteur's request. Another teacher at the École Normale Supérieure, Antoine-Jérôme Balard, agreed to hire Pasteur as a graduate laboratory assistant. Pasteur accepted.

Balard was among the greatest teachers at the university. In 1826, when he was only a twenty-four-year-old chemistry teacher, he discovered the element bromine, a dark-color liquid used today in medicines. As a result of this brilliant discovery, Balard was considered to be one of the top scientists in France. He was happy to take Pasteur under his wing, because he saw the great potential in this focused, serious young scientist.

THE SCIENCE OF CRYSTALS

As a lab assistant one of Pasteur's jobs was to create research projects for himself and the lab to work on. One of the subjects that interested

Pasteur was a branch of chemistry called crystallography, which was the study of the crystalline structure of materials. Crystallography was an exciting, new field in Pasteur's time. Scholars had begun to theorize that many chemicals were built of crystals on the molecular level, but the role of crystals in living matter was not fully understood. Pasteur believed that by studying crystals he could gain more knowledge in chemistry. Now he had to devise a project.

He was intrigued by a finding made by the famous German crystallographer and chemist Eilhardt Mitscherlich, who said that tartaric and racemic acids, two common chemicals, were identical in composition but different in their ability to rotate light. This phenomenon, that substances with the same chemical

Antoine Jerome Balard, a French chemist, discovered the element bromium.

composition can have different properties, is called isomerism. This gave Pasteur the idea for his research. He would try to find out why light behaved differently in two chemicals that were otherwise identical in every way.

MIRROR CRYSTALS

Tartaric acid was a common chemical in Pasteur's day. It was a by-product of the wine-making process and was used in the dying of textiles, so it was produced in large quantities for industrial use. Tartaric acid was usually sold as big, milky crystals. In 1819, scientists discovered racemic acid. Later it was discovered to be a second form of tartaric acid. Although it was determined that the two chemicals were identical, several experiments had shown that polarized light did not behave the same in the two chemicals. Tartaric acid rotated light, while racemic acid seemed to have no effect on light. This was astonishing because if the two chemicals were indeed identical, light should behave the same in both.

Pasteur decided to study both chemicals thoroughly to find the difference between them. Soon he discovered something no other scientist had noticed. The molecular crystals, or isomers, in tartaric acid were right-handed, while the crystals of racemic acid contained both right- and left-handed forms. They were mirror images of each other. He conducted more experiments, separating the different crystal compounds, and then tested these separate compounds with polarized light. Sure enough, the right-handed crystals rotated light to the right, while the left-handed crystals rotated light to the left.

What, exactly, had Pasteur discovered? He now had proof that a molecule could exist in two forms, one right-handed and the other left-handed. The idea is similar to that of a person looking into a mirror. The reflection in the mirror is identical to the person, but they are opposite of one another. He showed that asymmetry existed in crystals, which no other scientist had done before. He realized that, in general, this asymmetry was only present in organic compounds that had once been living organisms. Tartaric acid, part of the wine-making process, was organic. Minerals, such as quartz, were not organic, and they did not show the same kind of asymmetry. Pasteur's discovery came to be known as molecular asymmetry.

These were all enormous discoveries, especially for a

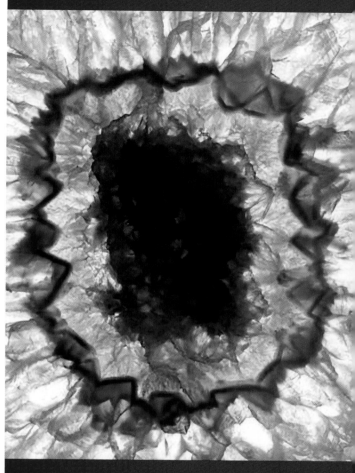

During Pasteur's research, he discovered that some crystals had both left- and right-handed forms. This discovery is known as molecular asymmetry.

young, unknown graduate student. Pasteur understood what he had found, and legend says that, unable to contain his excitement on the day of his discovery, he rushed out of the lab, ran into an instructor from the university, and immediately dragged him back to the lab to see his work.

THE CRYSTALS PASS A TEST

Pasteur was so excited about his discovery that he wanted to write a paper about his findings and publish it in a scientific journal immediately. But his mentor, Balard, cautioned against it. He knew that older, more experienced scientists might not accept the findings of this upstart young man. Instead, he suggested that Pasteur contact one of the greatest scientific minds in France, Jean-Baptiste Biot, a physicist and mathematician. If he could convince Biot of his findings, then the scientific community would certainly embrace the new discoveries.

Pasteur agreed, and Biot accepted. A few weeks later, in the spring of 1848, Pasteur found himself in the presence of the great scientist. Biot watched as Pasteur prepared his experiments. Sometimes Biot prepared parts of the experiment as well. Then they watched the polarized light rotate exactly the way Pasteur had said it would. The older scientist was astonished by the great discovery. He told Pasteur that this discovery stirred his heart.

Soon afterward, Pasteur's discoveries were published in the report of the Academy of Sciences, the most respected scientific organization in France at the time. A few months later Biot himself announced the discovery to a gathering of the academy, saying that Pasteur's discovery would have "the most fruitful applications in the future."

THE IMPORTANCE OF PASTEUR'S DISCOVERY

This discovery had enormous implications for the study of science, although many people did not know it at the time. Pasteur's work with crystals showed that two substances could be identical in composition but not alike in structure. He also made the connection between chemistry and biology, which until that time had not been linked. Most scientists considered them to be separate sciences with no connections. Now, science began to understand that living beings were constructed of molecules that were formed by unique chemical processes.

His discoveries would one day help unlock other mysteries of science in biology, chemistry, and medicine. In many ways, his work with crystals launched modern biology.

Jean-Baptiste Biot, a French physicist and mathematician, studied the relationship between electrical current and magnetism, as well as the polarization of light passing through chemical solutions.

Once Pasteur made his discovery of asymmetry in crystals, he began to receive attention and respect from well-known scientists.

CHAPTER FOUR

New Theories, New Discoveries

The year 1848 was a remarkable one for Pasteur. It was the year in which he made his discoveries about asymmetry in crystals. Once he had convinced Biot that his ideas were sound, the older scientist became Pasteur's supporter and mentor. As a result, other scientists began looking at Pasteur's work. With Biot's blessing and respect, Pasteur was convinced that achieving fame was just around the corner.

But that year was also filled with sorrow for Pasteur. In May, Pasteur got terrible news. His beloved mother was very sick. Pasteur dropped everything and rushed home to Arbois, but he was too late. She died of a stroke right before her only son arrived.

Pasteur was filled with guilt, both for not being with his mother before she died and for having chosen to live in Paris, so far away from home. Jean-Joseph was grief-stricken, too. He and his daughters pressured Louis to leave Paris and move closer to home. Louis Pasteur was torn between the love of his family and the love of science. He eventually agreed that if a university job closer to home was unavailable, he would take a less prestigious position at a smaller school.

EXILED TO THE PROVINCES

Pasteur was drifting and unclear about his next move. His graduate position was ending, his mother had died, and he had tasted a measure of success with his experiments with crystals. As his laboratory position ended, he waited for word as to where he would be assigned next.

He was informed that there was no position available in his field at any university or college in France. Instead, he would have to accept a position at a secondary school in Dijon. Pasteur was aghast at the thought of teaching high-school aged students. The schools were generally overcrowded, and he would have no time to conduct his own experiments. As with everything else he did, however, Pasteur became determined to be the best teacher he could be.

Pasteur hated teaching in Dijon. He became frustrated when he had to explain simple scientific concepts over and over to roomfuls of rowdy boys. He had no one to discuss science with and no time to continue his exciting research on crystals. Pasteur was convinced that all he needed to do was to hit upon a few more brilliant discoveries, publish them, and the scientific community would embrace him.

In the meantime, his mentor Balard was trying to find a better position for Pasteur somewhere closer to Paris. As the months wore on, Pasteur became so fed up with Dijon that he was ready to go back to Paris without a job. Then, in January 1849, Pasteur got some very good news. He had been offered a position as acting professor of chemistry at the University of Strasbourg. Pasteur packed his bags and left Dijon immediately, not even bothering to wait for his replacement at the secondary school.

BRIGHT OPPORTUNITIES AND NEW DREAMS

Pasteur arrived in Strasbourg in January 1849. Strasbourg was a midsize city known for its academics and industry. Pasteur was especially excited, for he had begun to imagine that he could find industrial uses for his scientific ideas. He wrote that Strasbourg was a town with many resources for chemistry, which suited him perfectly.

The students of Strasbourg were also interested in chemistry and the idea that it might have industrial applications, so Pasteur's lectures were well attended. What he loved most was that he could focus on the subjects that interested him, concentrating for weeks at a time if he wished. Pasteur had found a place that fit him well. He remained in Strasbourg for five years and did much important scientific work there.

PASTEUR FALLS IN LOVE

Immediately after Pasteur's arrival in Strasbourg, he met the new rector of the university, Charles Laurent. It didn't take Pasteur long to discover that

Laurent had two unmarried daughters, one named Marie. It is unclear when or where he met Marie, but it is certain that about a month after he arrived in Strasbourg, he asked Laurent for Marie's hand in marriage. After several months of waiting, Pasteur finally received a response. Marie agreed to marry Louis. They were married on May 29, 1849.

The city of Strasbourg, founded in 12 B.C., was a crossroads for many European travelers throughout history. This city has both French and German influences.

Little is known about Marie. She was born on January 15, 1826, and was twenty-three years old when she married Pasteur. Writers describe her as charming, kind, and demure. She understood that science would always come first in Pasteur's life. Marie saw her role as that of an assistant and helper, keeping their house and making sure Pasteur had enough time for his studies.

Louis and Marie soon began a family. Their first child, a daughter named Jeanne, was born in April 1850. Eighteen months later they welcomed a son, Jean-Baptiste. The Pasteurs eventually added three more children to the family: Cecile in 1853, Marie-Louise in 1858, and Camille in 1863.

ANOTHER BREAKTHROUGH WITH CRYSTALS

In 1851, the Pharmacy Society of Paris had announced a competition. Scientists were invited to find out if racemic acid could be created from tartaric acid. In other words, the task was to find out whether racemic acid could be artificially produced. Pasteur, feeling confident that he knew almost everything about tartaric acid, decided to try.

First, Pasteur reviewed some of the projects he was already working on. Part of his ongoing experiments with crystals included testing all kinds of chemicals. He was particularly interested in a drug known as quinine, which had been discovered in 1820. Quinine, along with other drugs called cinchonine and quinidine, was developed from the bark of the cinchona tree from South America. All of the drugs were very similar, and all were known to reduce fevers, but scientists did not fully understand their molecular compositions.

A Traditional Proposal

As was the custom in Pasteur's time, he wrote to Marie's father, Charles Laurent, asking permission to marry his daughter. The letter is one of the few examples of Pasteur's personal feelings and thoughts and gives the reader a touching glimpse of the kind of man Pasteur was.

The letter begins with Pasteur explaining that he is the son of a tanner from Arbois and describes his family. He then admits that he has no fortune or wealth to give to Laurent's daughter. Instead, he writes, "All I possess is good health, a kind heart, and my position in the University." Finally, he tells Laurent that his ambition is to gain recognition in science and return to Paris. He ends the letter with, "Please be assured, Monsieur, of my profound respect and devotion."

Pasteur began working with all three and soon discovered that quinidine was the right-handed isomer of quinine. He also discovered that heating the substances reduced their chemical stability and changed their molecular structures.

Then he returned to tartaric acid. He already knew that the way tartaric acid affected light changed when it was heated. Pasteur then had a burst of insight. He combined tartaric acid and cinchonine then heated them. To his delight and amazement, the cinchonine stabilized the mix, and the tartaric acid was transformed into racemic acid.

When he published his findings he created a sensation. He won the 1,500-franc prize from the Pharmacy Society of Paris in November

1853. This was a great deal of money, and Pasteur immediately used half of it to buy new equipment for his lab at the University of Strasbourg. For the second time, Pasteur had impressed the scientific world with his work on crystals.

His happiness was tempered by more bad news from home. His sister Emile died in 1853. His sister Josephine had passed away in 1850. Jean-Joseph was old and ill, and the losses in his family weighed on him. His son's work had become far too complex for him to understand. He accused Louis of abandoning him, which bothered Louis greatly. But Pasteur, only thirty years old, would not let the personal problems of his family keep him from moving forward with his career.

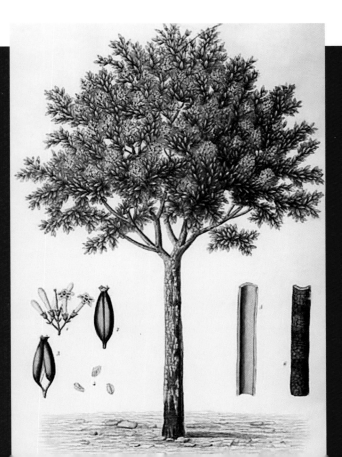

Quinine, cinchonine, and quinidine are all drugs that come from the bark of the cinchona tree (right). Pasteur used these substances in his experiments on changing molecular structure.

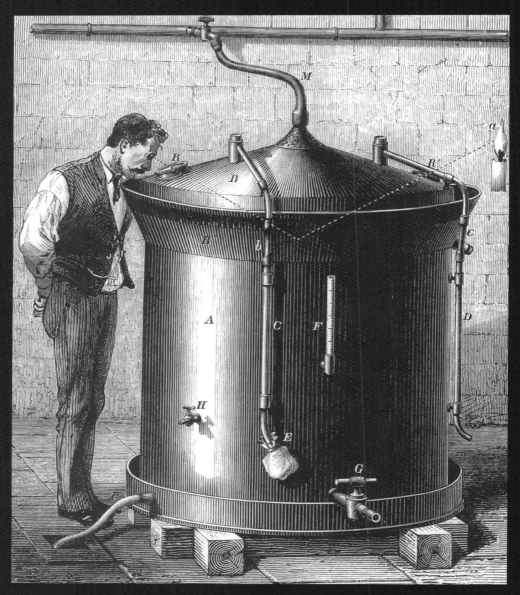

This large apparatus aided in the cooling and fermenting process of making beer.

CHAPTER FIVE

The Science of Fermentation

*P*asteur always believed in the saying "chance favors those who are prepared," and by 1854, he was very prepared to take whatever chances came his way. That year, based in large part on his successes with racemic acid, he was appointed to a position at the University of Lille, one of the most prestigious universities in France. The appointment was all the more sweet for Pasteur because it also included the deanship of the brand-new college of the sciences. In the fall of 1854, the Pasteurs moved to Lille.

LILLE: A CITY OF INDUSTRY AND SCIENCE

The choice to put the science college at the University of Lille had been made carefully by the French government. Lille was a bustling industrial city, the fifth largest city in France at the time. The town, once a medieval walled city, saw great growth in the 1800s. The city began to embrace new inventions and industries, such as chemical production, coal mining, distilling of beet juice to make a type of alcohol, brewing, and textile manufacturing.

The University of Lille reflected this acceptance of change and progress by focusing its energies on science, which excited Pasteur. In the past, most universities had focused only on traditional subjects, such as languages, history, and mathematics. In the 1800s, science became a new facet of education. At the same time, the rise of great industries showed that there was a need for bright, scientific minds to continue

Pasteur and the Potato

On December 7, 1854, Pasteur delivered his first lecture at the University of Lille. In it, he launched his ideas about how science could benefit industry and humanity. He became known for this attitude throughout the rest of his scientific career. He said, "Where will you find a young man whose interest and curiosity will not be aroused when you give him a potato and teach him to make it into sugar, and this sugar into alcohol, and this alcohol into ether and vinegar? Will he not be happy to tell his family at the end of the day that he operated an electric telegraph? And gentlemen, you can be sure that once such things are learned, they are rarely, perhaps never forgotten!"

creating the inventions and understanding how the science behind the various industries worked. So the decision to put a prestigious science program in the city made perfect sense. Science students at Lille were expected to prepare themselves for their scientific careers through a combination of academic courses and practical work in industry.

PASTEUR SHAKES UP LILLE

Pasteur taught chemistry classes, guiding budding scientists through the complex and new ideas of chemistry research. He also began to develop many new classes to help fellow professors create more science classes that could be linked to the industries of the town.

Pasteur encouraged professors to explore new ways of doing things. This spirit of creativity lured hundreds of excited students to Lille. The

Lille, one of the largest cities in northern France, is known for manufacturing textiles, transportation, and architecture.

school began offering evening courses in different scientific subjects, attracting workers and women from the city. Students went on field trips to the factories and companies throughout Lille, watching blast furnaces and fermentation vats at work, and learning firsthand how scientific concepts were used in manufacturing.

Pasteur believed strongly that he had to set an example, both for the students and for his fellow professors. He worked relentlessly, spending his days either lecturing in class or at the laboratory and continuing to pursue his own work during off hours.

Pasteur even set up a rudimentary lab in his home. Marie would sometimes come downstairs in the middle of the night to see the blue glow of the flames from the gas lights shining on Pasteur's concentrating face.

"MYSTERIOUS CHARACTER" OF FERMENTATION

One day early in 1856, Pasteur received a visitor. Mr. Bigo was an industrialist from Lille. His son Emile was taking Pasteur's classes at the Faculty of Sciences. Bigo had come to ask Pasteur's advice on a troubling problem.

He explained that many manufacturers of beet-root alcohol, an alcohol made from sugar beets, were having problems with their product. The alcohol either had an acidic taste or the fermentation vats where the sugar-beet liquid turned into alcohol gave off terrible smells. Bigo had heard many good things about Pasteur from his son and other manufacturers in town. He asked for his help.

Pasteur immediately agreed. He would find out what was going wrong with the alcohol and hopefully find a way to fix it.

What Is Fermentation?

Fermentation is a process in which an organic substance is broken down or converted to other substances by organisms such as bacteria, fungi, and yeast. Scientists in the 1800s did not understand how this worked, however, they did realize that there were several kinds of fermentation. Alcoholic fermentation was the best known. In alcoholic fermentation, sugars in a substance, such as grape juice, are transformed into alcohol, making products such as wine.

Other types of fermentation include acetic fermentation, which results in an acid or vinegar product. Lactic fermentation yields lactic acid, which makes milk sour. Putrid fermentation, or putrefaction, is responsible for the rotten, stinking smell of spoiled meat and eggs.

Pasteur was unsure about leaving his work with crystals and turning his attention to fermentation. He finally decided that the unanswered questions about fermentation were too interesting to ignore. Also, he was excited by the chance to use his scientific knowledge to help industry, just as he encouraged his students to do.

THE UNKNOWNS ABOUT FERMENTATION

Scientists throughout history had studied fermentation. It was known that yeast had something to do with the process. When Pasteur took up the problem, there were still many unanswered questions about the process. For instance, no one knew exactly why grape juice bubbled in the fermentation vats, or why alcohol sometimes turned into vinegar, as was the problem with Lille's beet-root alcohol manufacturers.

Scientists were aware that yeast were living organisms that had something to do with fermentation. Some scientists thought the motion of the yeast caused fermentation. Others thought fermentation created yeast. Still others speculated that it was the decomposition of yeast that caused fermentation. A few scientists had shown that oxygen and other chemicals may have something to do with fermentation, but none of their experiments were conclusive.

A NEW PERSPECTIVE ON AN OLD QUESTION

Pasteur decided to tackle the problem from the perspective of biology. If yeasts were living organisms, he reasoned, then the process by which fermentation occurred could have something to do with their biology rather than with a chemical process or reaction.

He began to experiment with lactic acid, which causes milk to ferment and turn sour. He guessed that the fermentation was being caused by lactic yeast and was finally able to see them through a microscope.

In the 1850s, scientists knew little about the fermentation process. Using this apparatus, Pasteur conducted many experiments about the biology of fermentation.

Other scientists had missed them because they are very small.

He also reasoned that yeast needed nutrients, or food, to multiply and cause fermentation. Pasteur added nutrients to the milk, and sure enough, the milk soured and fermented. He was eventually able to grow the yeast and control the fermentation process.

He had not answered the main question, however. What caused fermentation? Now that he was convinced fermentation was a biological process, and because he had successfully isolated lactic yeast, he was ready to tackle the biggest question: What caused alcoholic fermentation?

STRANGE YEASTS

During Pasteur's earlier experiments, he had looked at wine through a microscope. He noticed that properly aged wine contained small, round cells. He rightly realized that these were yeast cells. But in sour wine, these cells looked different. They were elongated. Something was causing the microorganisms in the vats to take a different shape, and Pasteur guessed that whatever made that happen was probably the same thing that made wine go sour.

Another puzzle about yeasts and fermentation concerned oxygen. Earlier scientists had discovered that if oxygen was present during some stages of the fermentation process, the alcohol would go bad. Scientists used this phenomenon as proof that fermentation was a chemical process.

Through experimentation, Pasteur made an astounding, two-fold discovery. Yeast were indeed living organisms, but they did not need oxygen to live. He began to focus his study on the yeast themselves and soon made some startling discoveries.

PASTEUR TURNS SCIENCE UPSIDE DOWN

Once Pasteur focused his study on yeast, all of the answers became clear. He discovered that fermentation occurred when the living yeast reproduced. He was able to point to the things that had to be present for yeast to reproduce and then for fermentation to occur. Pasteur also proved that adding nitrogen-rich compounds to a fermenting product would spur the yeasts to feed, reproduce, and cause fermentation.

His most masterful stroke of genius, however, was to show that the problems with fermentation were caused by the presence of different microorganisms. For instance, sour wine was created when bacteria or other organisms contaminated the fermentation vats. In the case of the beet-juice alcohol manufacturers, Pasteur showed that the vats had been contaminated with lactic yeast, the yeast present in sour milk. He suggested that the manufacturers heat the beet juice slightly, just enough to kill the microorganisms. Then they could restart the fermentation process with fresh, healthy brewer's yeast. This idea of heating a substance to kill the impurities was revolutionary. The process became known as pasteurization.

PASTEUR'S REVOLUTION

It is difficult to underestimate Pasteur's astounding discoveries about fermentation. He did more than solve a problem for a few manufacturing plants. His discoveries rocked the scientific world by combining his knowledge of chemistry and biology to show that these two scientific disciplines interacted in significant ways.

In the 1800s, most scientists were convinced that each branch of science was its own world with its own rules. Pasteur was the first scientist to prove that all the branches of science were interconnected.

Pasteur showed that the fermentation of alcohol was related to the souring of milk and the spoiling of food by showing how different living microorganisms behaved. His identification of lactic yeast was the first time a scientist had identified a microorganism. Although a few scientists didn't believe Pasteur's conclusions, the majority hailed his discoveries. In 1859, even before he published a paper on his findings, the Academy of Sciences awarded him a prize for experimental physiology.

Pasteur's discovery of microorganisms literally created the science of microbiology. Most of his later work would be in this new and exciting field of study.

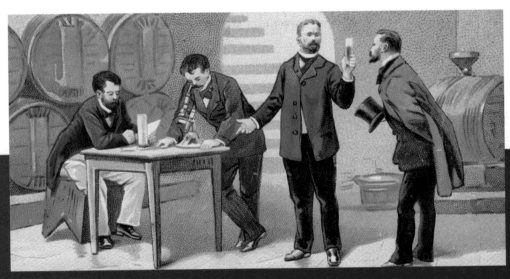

This is an advertising card for the Chocolaterie d'Aiguebelle promoting Pasteur's discovery of pasteurization.

Pasteur performed experiments to prove that tiny living things in the air caused fermentation and putrefaction and that heating these organisms would kill them.

CHAPTER SIX

Spontaneous Generation

*P*asteur knew that, although his work had been universally cheered, he was still considered a provincial scientist from an insignificant university. To be respected, he had to work in Paris. He got a big break in October 1857, when he was appointed administrator and director of scientific studies of the École Normale Supérieure. His dream had finally come true. A few weeks later the Pasteur family arrived in Paris.

FAILURE AMIDST SUCCESS

During the two years Pasteur worked on fermentation, a rare opportunity had presented itself. A spot in the prestigious Academy of Sciences had become available, and Pasteur was determined to get it.

To become a member of the Academy of Sciences, one had to be voted on favorably by the existing members. To get their good will and their votes, Pasteur had made frequent trips to Paris, abandoning his fermentation experiments to meet the members and ask for their votes.

Pasteur, however, had several strikes against him. First, he didn't live in Paris. This was against the rules, and exceptions were only made for celebrated and respected scientists. Pasteur was not yet either. Also, the spot that had opened up was reserved for a geologist, and Pasteur was a crystallographer.

This illustration shows the artist's idealized view of the Academy of Sciences and Fine Arts. The members of the Academy are dressed in classical garb to indicate their learnedness and to emphasize the ties of learning to the ancient world.

Pasteur did his best. He prepared a letter of resignation to the University of Lille to show the academy that he was serious about moving to Paris should he be chosen. He also had many supporters, including Biot, who campaigned strongly for him. In the end, however, he lost the election.

He took the news well publicly, saying that he was glad the election process had made him and his work better known to the scientists in the academy. Privately, he was bitterly disappointed.

A SORRY EXCUSE FOR A SCHOOL

The École Normale Supérieure that Pasteur came to in 1857 was nothing like the grand school he had attended as a student. Although it continued to have a good reputation, its quality had been declining for several years. Pasteur noted that it was only a shadow of its former self when he arrived.

Pasteur was put in charge of scientific studies at the school. But that turned out to be only a small part of his job. Pasteur's more important task was to oversee economic and sanitary conditions, and discipline, as well as be the liaison between the school and the students' families.

Pasteur became concerned about everything from where the school's food was coming from to making sure structural repairs were done to the school's buildings. Although he meant well, his aloof style and autocratic way of giving orders put people off. When he gave an order, he expected to be obeyed and became very upset if someone did something he thought was against the rules. It didn't take long for Pasteur to become intensely disliked by both the student body and the

"I Have Grown Accustomed to My Attic"

In June 1858, a few months after Pasteur's arrival at the École Normale Supérieure, he wrote to his friend Mr. Chappius about his work. He continued to conduct fermentation experiments in his attic, and he described how uncomfortable it was, saying, "I should be pursuing the consequences of these facts, if a temperature of 36°C (96.8°F) did not keep me from my laboratory. I regret to see the longest days in the year lost to me. Yet I have grown accustomed to my attic, and I should be sorry to leave it. . . . You too are struggling against material hindrances in your work; let it stimulate us, my dear fellow, not discourage us. Our discoveries will have the greater merit."

administration of the school. Although he worked hard, he was never the beloved professor he had once been at Lille.

A LAB IN THE ATTIC

Pasteur was anxious to continue his studies on fermentation at the university, but he soon realized that the school had no money or space to build a laboratory for him. He found a hot, cramped attic space that no one else wanted. There was no money for equipment, so Pasteur bought his own. He also had to pay for the supplies he needed for his experiments. Pasteur was undeterred. He would continue his experiments, no matter what it took.

Soon the school, perhaps embarrassed that it had forced a respected scientist to build a lab in an unused attic, offered Pasteur a small out-building once used by the architecture department. Pasteur accepted the new space, even though it was little better than the attic had been. The space would later be enlarged somewhat, but it would never be the grand lab that Pasteur needed. It was there that Pasteur began to tackle the question of spontaneous generation.

THE THEORY OF SPONTANEOUS GENERATION

For centuries, scientists and thinkers had tried to discover where life came from. Do living things always come from other living things? Or are there other ways that life begins? Ancient scientists had to rely on their observations to create theories of why things happened.

Many believed that living things could come from nonliving things. For instance, people noticed that when meat rotted, tiny white maggots appeared in the meat. The maggots then turned into flies. This led them to believe that the flies were created from the meat. They did not realize that flies laid eggs on the meat, which hatched into more flies. This theory that living things can arise from nonliving matter is known as the theory of spontaneous generation. Spontaneous generation was a well-respected theory held by the most prominent scientists in history.

Not every scientist believed in spontaneous generation. In 1668, an Italian scientist named Francesco Redi conducted an experiment to see if flies really did come from rotting meat. He put meat in several jars, then covered some of the jars. After a few days, Redi saw maggots on the meat in the open jars. The meat in the covered jars did not have any

A Recipe for Making Mice

One of the most famous examples of the belief in spontaneous generation comes from a seventeenth-century Flemish scientist named Jan van Helmont. He wrote a description, or recipe, of how one could spontaneously generate mice in jar. He stated, "If you press a piece of underwear soiled with sweat together with some wheat in an open mouth jar, after about 21 days the odor changes and the ferment [odor] coming out of the underwear . . . changes the wheat to mice. But what is more remarkable is that fully grown mice of both sexes emerge from the wheat."

Van Helmont gave other recipes for spontaneous generation, such as "The fumes which rise from the bottom of a swamp produce frogs, ants, leeches, and vegetation." Also, "carve an indentation in a brick, fill it with crushed basil, and cover the brick with another so that the indentation is completely sealed. Expose the two bricks to sunlight and you will find that within a few days fumes from the basil . . . will have transformed the vegetable matter into scorpions."

Jan van Helmont is famous for his recipes for spontaneous generation of animals such as mice and frogs.

maggots. For a time, the idea of spontaneous generation began to fall from favor. Ironically, however, it was the invention and use of the microscope that brought the idea of spontaneous generation back into scientific respectability.

When scientists began viewing things under microscopes, they saw tiny organisms swimming everywhere. These organisms reproduced rapidly without mating. Scientists began to support the idea that, although spontaneous generation did not work to produce large animals such as mice, it did create microscopic organisms. This was the prevailing scientific thought until the 1800s, when Pasteur disproved it.

PASTEUR AND THE SWAN-NECKED FLASKS

Many of the experiments Pasteur had conducted with fermentation, such as heating to kill bacteria, pointed him to the idea that spontaneous

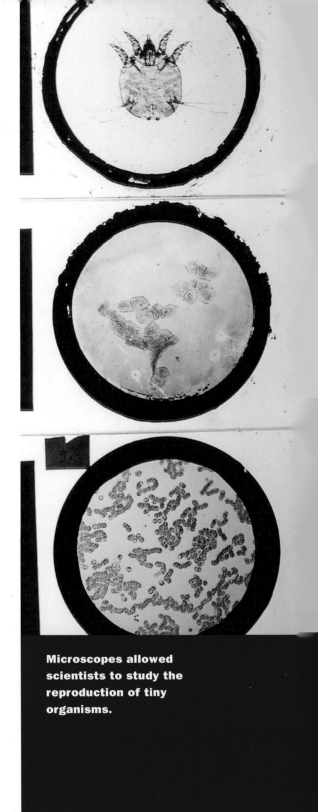

Microscopes allowed scientists to study the reproduction of tiny organisms.

Chicken Broth and the Life Force

In the mid–1700s, an Englishman named John Needham who believed in spontaneous generation theorized that a "life force" was present in all nonliving things, and this life force was what caused new organisms to spring to life. He conducted an experiment to prove his idea. Needham boiled chicken broth for a few minutes, put the broth into a flask, and sealed the flask with a cork. A few days later the broth was teeming with microorganisms. Needham said this proved that spontaneous generation existed.

An Italian scientist, Lazzaro Spallanzani, was not convinced. He argued that the microorganisms had survived the boiling or found their way into the broth after it was boiled. He conducted his own experiments, boiling the chicken broth for an hour before sealing it in a flask by melting the flask opening shut. Nothing grew in the broth. Then he put some of the broth into a flask that was sealed with a cork. Bacteria grew in this broth.

Spallanzani concluded that air had been able to get into the cork-sealed flask, carrying with it bacteria that contaminated the broth. He therefore proved that spontaneous generation was false. Needham was furious, arguing that it was the "life force" in the air that made the bacteria spontaneously generate in the cork-sealed flasks.

As the debate raged, each scientist had his supporters. By 1860, the argument had grown so fierce that the Paris Academy of Sciences offered a prize to anyone who could create an experiment that would settle the issue once and for all. It was Pasteur who finally claimed the prize in 1864.

generation was false. Pasteur knew he needed to do very detailed, specific experiments to disprove the idea of spontaneous generation once and for all. So he decided to set up his experiments in phases.

The first step was to prove that microorganisms were in the air and not created by spontaneous generation. He invented a small vacuum machine that pulled air from the outside then filtered it through a wad of sterile material. Pasteur rinsed the material then looked at the water in the magnifying glass. Sure enough, it was teeming with microorganisms. The next step was to show that these microorganisms reproduced. Through a series of experiments with water and sealed flasks, he was able to do this also.

His next step was to show that the fewer microorganisms, or germs, that are deposited in the liquid, the more the liquid will remain sterile. This is the moment when Pasteur had a burst of intuition. He needed some kind of vessel that was open to the outside air but would, in some way, keep the germs in the air from getting inside. He created several large, long-necked flasks. The

Lazzaro Spallanzani, an Italian physiologist, attacked the theories of spontaneous generation set up by John Needham.

necks on these vessels were thin, and they rose, fell, twisted, and bent back on themselves somewhat like a swan's neck. The twists and turns allowed air to get inside, but germs would be trapped in the bends of the neck. His experiments worked. The liquid in the swan-necked flasks stayed pure and free of microorganisms. When he tipped a flask to allow the pure liquid to touch a bend in the neck and then returned the liquid to the flask, the liquid became contaminated.

Other scientists weren't convinced, so Pasteur decided to collect air from the purest places in the world, places he believed fewer germs lived. He wanted to prove that if a liquid is exposed to the purest possible air, no spontaneous generation would take place. He traveled to the Alps, one of the world's highest mountain ranges. He took dozens of water-filled flasks with him. On the mountaintops he opened the flasks to the air, then

This flask was used by Pasteur during his experiments. The thin neck twists so air is allowed in, but not germs.

resealed them by melting the glass necks so that no other air could get in.

Once he was back in Paris, he broke open the flasks that he had taken to the mountain. The liquid was not contaminated. However, when he broke open flasks that had been filled with air from Paris and other areas, the liquid was teeming with microorganisms. Pasteur had proven that microorganisms traveled through the air, and that spontaneous generation did not exist. He won the academy's prize for disproving the theory of spontaneous generation.

Most of the scientific community was convinced, still not all scientists agreed with Pasteur's findings. There continued to be arguments between those who supported Pasteur and those who wanted to believe in spontaneous generation. Pasteur savored his success. With this discovery, his place as a great scientist was assured.

Pasteur traveled to the Alps, where he believed the purest air was, to conduct his experiment to disprove spontaneous generation.

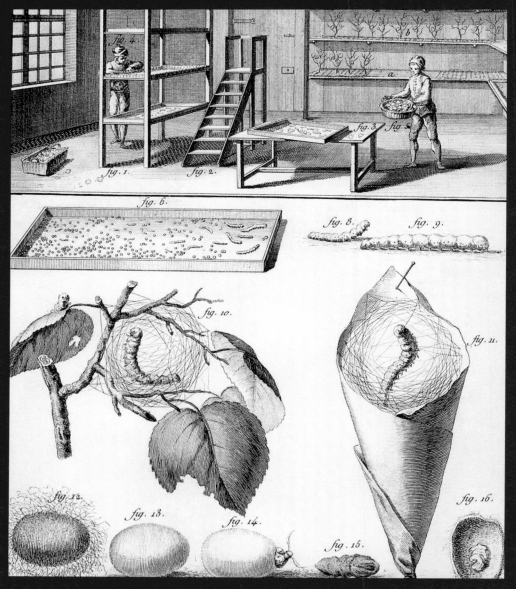

The illustration represents a diagram of the silkworm's life cycle and a silkmaking operation.

CHAPTER SEVEN

Why Are the Silkworms Dying?

*P*asteur's experiments with spontaneous generation lasted from the time he arrived at the École Normale Supérieure until the early 1860s. That time was to be one of the most significant in his life, not only for the successes he saw, but for the personal tragedies he endured.

SUCCESS AND SORROW

In the summer of 1862, Pasteur learned of an opening in the mineralogy section of the Academy of Sciences. This time, Pasteur was determined to win the spot. His friend and supporter Biot had died, and there were still many members of the academy who didn't want Pasteur to become a member. His enemies worked hard against him, but Pasteur wouldn't be put off so easily. At one point he built wooden models of right- and left-handed tartaric acid, then called a special session to defend his work. He argued his ideas on molecular asymmetry so well that in the end, the academy was convinced. He was elected to the Academy of Sciences in December of 1862.

The next year Pasteur received a special request from the ruler of France. He was asked by Napoléon III to study wine diseases. In 1864, he set up a laboratory in Arbois for this work.

Between the years 1859 and 1866, Pasteur suffered great losses in his family. In August 1859, his oldest daughter, Jeanne, died of typhoid fever. Two beloved family members, his father Jean-Joseph and his

Pasteur pictured with his wife, Marie. Pasteur experienced the loss of his father and three daughters between 1859 and 1866.

Pasteur's Grief

After Jeanne's death, Pasteur wrote an eloquent description of the terrible grief he suffered. He said, "I heard the sound of the coffin and of the cords that took it down to the bottom of her grave, and the sound of the earth falling on that wood, both so empty and so full. . . . What are those letters from strangers, from friends, even family? Vain talk—drops of water taken from the fury of the ocean."

daughter Camille, died within three months of one another in 1865. And in 1866, his daughter Cecile also died of typhoid fever.

Pasteur, usually in such command of himself, was devastated by the deaths of his children and his father. He was bitter and stunned that modern medicine could do nothing to help them. His only solace was his work and his remaining two children, Jean-Baptiste and Marie-Louise. He wrote to Marie that he was glad of their love, their love for their children and their future, and his dreams of science. He went on to say that he hoped he could make their lives beautiful through his work and his new discoveries.

In 1865, Pasteur was forty-three years old. He had risen from an unknown provincial scientist to become one of the most prominent young scientists in France and perhaps the world. His position as the director of scientific studies at the École Normale Supérieure was among the most prestigious jobs in the country. He had experience in several scientific areas, including crystallography, chemistry, and biology.

He was still as opinionated, fiery, and stubborn as he had been as a young student. He used all of these qualities as he tackled his next huge scientific question—a question that arrived one day in the mail.

"MISERY IS GREATER HERE"

In the spring of 1865, Pasteur's old friend and former professor, Jean-Baptiste Dumas, wrote him a letter. Dumas had risen far since his days as a professor, and by that year he was a senator in the French government. His particular interests lay with France's silk industry. Something was terribly wrong with the silkworms that produced the fine silk fibers used to make silk cloth. The silkworms were dying. Dumas's letter described the plight of the silkworm breeders, saying that "misery is greater here than anything one can imagine." He asked Pasteur if he would help find out what was happening to the worms.

At first, Pasteur was hesitant. He was not a biologist, and he didn't have a clue about silkworms. He told Dumas that he couldn't help, but Dumas persisted. He told Pasteur that France needed his help. It was a plea that Pasteur could not ignore. It was a new and interesting challenge, and Pasteur always liked new challenges. He agreed. He would spend the next six years, from 1865 to 1871, studying the silkworm and trying to figure out the problem.

A STRANGE DISEASE

By the 1800s, silk production was one of the largest industries in France. Plantations all over the country bred silkworms and produced thousands

Silkworms to Silk

Most of the beautiful, lustrous silk fiber used around the world comes from a small worm—the caterpillar or larva of the silkworm moth. Domestic silkworm breeders carefully raise the silkworms, feeding them mulberry leaves. The worms go through several body changes, or metamorphoses, until they are ready to spin their cocoons. The silk is the filament they use to make their cocoons. Once the worms have made these cocoons, the silkworm breeders kill the worms and then unspool the fine filaments of silk from the cocoons. After several industrial processes that prepare the filaments, they are then woven into silk fabric.

Some worms in the cocoons, or pupae, are allowed to live, so that the adult moths can emerge from their cocoons and mate. After mating, the females deposit eggs, called "seeds," which then hatch into a new batch of silkworms.

of bolts of cloth. Now, however, the breeding chambers seemed to be contaminated, and the disease appeared to be transmitted through the eggs themselves. At first the breeders simply ordered more silkworms from other countries, such as Spain or Italy, to replace the ones that died. Slowly the disease spread to those countries as well. By the time Pasteur began looking into the problem, the only country that could produce healthy eggs was Japan.

The disease was confusing because it had different effects. Most of the time, great numbers of silkworms died right after they hatched.

Others died during the early stages of their life cycles or stopped growing altogether. In some places, the silkworms survived but they became reddish in color, developed black spots, and would not spin cocoons. In other places, the worms seemed to survive to the point where they would start to spin cocoons, but instead of spinning, they would stop eating and die.

Everyone in the world who made a living from silk trading and producing became increasingly worried about the silkworm problem. Not only was Pasteur working for France, but his findings, whatever they would be, would have an impact on the whole world.

PASTEUR GETS TO WORK

The first thing Pasteur had to do was to become familiar with the silkworm industry. He read as much as he could about the life cycle of the silkworm. He decided that the best way to study the silkworm was to go to a town that had several silkworm facilities, so he moved to the small French town of Alès. Eventually his entire family, along with several assistants, would join him there.

He examined silkworm cocoons, spoke to breeders, and observed the plantations where the silkworms were bred and raised. He set up a workstation at a plantation to observe the silkworms each day, as they went through their life cycles.

Almost immediately he saw the symptoms of the disease. One of the most common symptoms were the black spots, called corpuscles, that appeared on the worms. Pasteur began to call the disease pebrine, a word that comes from the French word for pepper. Oddly, some of the worms that had pebrine did not get sick, and some healthy worms eventually produced black-spotted eggs. Pasteur was puzzled.

Pasteur spent hours at the plantation, examining worms, cocoons, and the pupae inside. He discovered that even when a worm seemed healthy, it was usually covered with spots when it became a pupa. Most of the time the adult moths were also full of corpuscles. Pasteur concluded that the black spots were a late-appearing symptom the disease.

Pasteur was wrong, but he wouldn't know it for several years. He conducted experiments and suggested conclusions, but none of them answered the question that was puzzling Pasteur most: Why did some healthy worms turn into black-spotted, diseased moths? He discounted factors such as diseased food as the cause of the corpuscles. Finally, he began to consider a different theory: That the spots were not a symptom, but one of the causes of the disease.

At first, Pasteur discounted this theory. Slowly, however, he began to

Silkworms go through many body changes until they are ready to spin their cocoons. The fibers of the cocoon are used to make silk.

realize that this might be the answer. He conducted a series of experiments and eventually concluded that the black spots were caused by a parasite. He fed healthy worms mulberry leaves contaminated with corpuscles. These worms immediately got sick. He also learned of an incident at a nearby silkworm farm in which a new batch of healthy worms from Japan became black-spotted moths. When Pasteur investigated, he saw that the healthy worms had been housed below a cage full of diseased and dead worms. He realized that the corpuscle material in the diseased cage had dropped down into the cage of healthy worms, contaminating them.

Pasteur had proved that the disease was contagious and transmitted by a parasite, but he didn't know exactly how the parasite transmitted the disease. Through additional experimentation, he discovered that there were several ways the disease spread. Eating corpuscle-tainted leaves was one way that worms got the disease. Another way was heredity, because diseased moths often laid infected eggs.

He eventually discovered that there were two separate diseases affecting the silkworms. Pebrine, caused the corpuscles that he saw on the worms, pupae, and moths. Pupae with pebrine often died in their cocoons. The second disease was known as flacherie. Worms with that disease had no spots but were unable to spin cocoons.

A LINK BETWEEN SILKWORMS AND FERMENTATION

Flacherie was causing Pasteur more headaches. That disease did not cause black spots, so it was probably not transmitted by the parasite that caused pebrine. So, what could be causing it?

One day Pasteur visited a silkworm farm that was infested with flacherie. He noticed a strong, unpleasant smell near the beds full of diseased worms. It reminded him a lot of the smell of fermentation. He knew that fermentation occurred because of microorganisms, so he wondered if this disease might be caused by microorganisms too.

He conducted experiments, looking at the worms and moths through a microscope and feeding them contaminated mulberry leaves. He saw bacteria in the intestines of the infected worms. He realized that these bacteria were the cause of the disease. He eventually came to understand that the bacteria multiplied in the intestines of healthy worms. This is how some worms could look healthy but actually be sick.

Pasteur discovered that silkworms were getting sick because they were feeding on contaminated mulberry leaves. He also proved that the disease was contagious and was transmitted by a parasite.

The droppings of these worms contaminated others and caused the smell that Pasteur had initially noticed. Pasteur had identified how bacteria infected a living animal, how it reproduced, and how it was transmitted.

THE SOLUTION TO THE PROBLEM

Pasteur had discovered the cause of the silkworms' disease. Now he had to figure out how to prevent it. He consulted the writings of successful Chinese and Japanese silkworm growers, who emphasized cleanliness and control of temperature. Pasteur proposed that cleanliness would be the best weapon against transmission of the disease because it was usually transmitted through contaminated food and silkworm beds. He suggested that nurseries be carefully scrubbed and cleaned, that the rooms be properly ventilated, that special attention be paid to keeping the mulberry leaves clean and uncontaminated, and that the temperature of the breeding chambers be regulated. And finally, he recommended that all diseased silkworms be destroyed.

Today, these preventative measures seem like ordinary, common-sense ideas. But the silkworm industry was furious. They didn't want to take the time and effort to implement these changes. They argued that Pasteur was wrong, and many jealous scientists agreed with them. Pasteur began to receive complaints from around France, along with stories of how his measures didn't work. Pasteur, with his usual arrogance, maintained that his ideas would work, and that anyone who experienced failure simply wasn't doing things correctly.

Merchants who had grown rich importing Japanese silkworms for France were Pasteur's worst enemies. They saw that their businesses would be destroyed by these new measures. If the disease was eradicated, there would no longer be a need for the importation of expensive, healthy Japanese silkworms. The merchants began to spread rumors that Pasteur's methods didn't work.

Eventually, however, the silkworm breeders began to implement Pasteur's suggestions. Slowly, through several silkworm-breeding seasons, they began to see results. By 1870, the cocoon harvest was better than it had been in years. Pasteur had solved the problem.

SILKWORMS START THE REVOLUTION

Pasteur's work with silkworms may have started as a way to help the silk industry, but his discoveries had a far-reaching effect on the world in many important ways. Pasteur concluded that such things as temperature, humidity, ventilation, quality of food, sanitation, and adequate separation of newly hatched worms played a role in their susceptibility to disease. This was the first step toward developing ideas about preventative medicine. The implications of this discovery were enormous. Pasteur's conclusions brought about new advances in several scientific fields, including medicine, microbiology, and, of course, the silkworm industry.

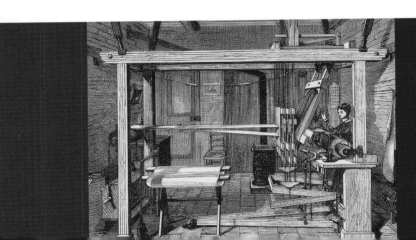

A woman operates a large silk-weaving loom in this engraving created in 1875.

Pasteur works with an early sterilizer that helped pioneer his work on diseases.

CHAPTER EIGHT

Pasteurization and the Germ Theory of Disease

By October 1868, Pasteur was in the middle of his research and experimentation on the silkworm problem and had asked to present a report on his studies to the Academy of Sciences. On the morning of October 19, the day he was to present his speech, he complained of a tingling sensation over the left side of his body. He shrugged it off, although Marie became alarmed. After lunchtime, he experienced a fit of shivering that forced him to bed, making Marie more worried. He insisted, however, on appearing for his afternoon appointment with the academy.

Pasteur gave his talk with a steady voice, then he went home, ate a light meal, and went to bed early. Almost as soon as he lay down, the strange symptoms returned and worsened. Soon he was unable to move his left side or speak. Marie sent an urgent message to Pasteur's personal physicians, Dr. Godelier and Dr. Gueneau de Mussy, who arrived immediately. They, along with a physician from the academy, Dr. Andral, bled him with leeches, which seemed to relieve the symptoms, but he soon became worse. Eventually Pasteur could barely move or speak, although his doctors noted that he had an active mind and wanted to talk about science.

Today's physicians would have immediately recognized that Pasteur was having a stroke, which is a sudden disruption of blood flow to the brain, caused by either a clot or a leak in a blood vessel. At the time, the

After his stroke, Pasteur had to rely on others to help him use his lab instruments.

medical community didn't know what caused this condition, and they were powerless to treat it.

For days, it was unclear whether Pasteur would live. His left side was paralyzed, and he could not speak at all. Prominent scientists from all over the country came to the Pasteur home. Slowly, Pasteur began to improve. His speech came back bit by bit. After a few weeks, he was well enough to sit in a chair, although his left side was still paralyzed.

By January 1869, Pasteur was able to walk again. He would eventually recover from his stroke, but he would never fully regain the use of his left side, and he would forever rely on others to help him with writing and experimenting. Marie became his most trusted personal assistant, writing letters for him and doing everything he could no longer do. It was in this condition that he completed his work on the silkworm problem, which became one of his greatest triumphs.

"The News Is Rather Good"

In 1868, a relative of the Pasteur family, Mrs. Criber, wrote a letter that described the atmosphere of the Pasteur home during the scientist's sudden illness. She wrote, "The news is rather good this morning; the patient was able to sleep for a few hours last night, which he had not done. . . . All scientific Paris comes to inquire anxiously after the patient; intimate friends take it in turns to watch by him. Dumas, the great chemist, was affectionately insisting on taking his turn yesterday. . . . His stroke is accompanied by symptoms which are now occupying the attention of the whole Academy of Medicine."

HEAT KILLS MICROORGANISMS

During the years Pasteur was working on the silkworm problem, he was also finishing up his work for Napoléon III. He had asked Pasteur if he would look into the problem with wine production. Pasteur was a natural choice for this assignment because of his work with fermentation.

Pasteur had decided to begin his studies of wine in his hometown of Arbois. Arbois was a wine-making town, and its local wines were well known in France. Pasteur assembled a team of scientists and students to help him. For three summers, 1863, 1864, and 1865, Pasteur studied vineyards, grapes, and wine.

Although Pasteur had grown up in wine country, this was the first time he had really studied the properties of wine and wine-making. There were several problems that could occur during wine production, all of which made the wine unfit to drink. Some made wine turn sour or bitter; others made the wine turn cloudy or oily, while others made the wine taste watery. Winemakers had all kinds of ideas about why these problems occurred, but no one knew exactly what caused them.

Pasteur suspected that the problems were caused by microorganisms present in the wine. He found several different types of microorganisms that made wine go bad. For instance, one came from rotten grapes. He also discovered the microorganism that caused wine to become bitter. Once he had discovered the culprits, he then had to figure out how to prevent the spoilage from occurring.

At that point, Pasteur remembered something from his experiments with fermentation. He recalled that heating killed the bacteria during fermentation. He also read about other scientists conducting successful experiments on preserving foods by either heating or freezing them. Pasteur realized that heating the wine might kill the microorganisms that caused the spoilage. His process was very simple. He heated the wine for a few minutes, without air. His experiment worked. He later obtained a patent for his idea, which he called "pasteurization."

At first, there was great opposition to Pasteur's idea of pasteurization. Most winemakers insisted that heating the wine would destroy its taste. Pasteur, sure of his conclusions and offended that anyone would dare to question his work, offered to conduct taste tests. The wine didn't lose its flavor. Once again, Pasteur saved an entire French industry.

During the summers of 1863, 1864, and 1865, Pasteur studied the process of wine-making. He discovered that heating the wine killed the microorganisms that

Soon after his discoveries pasteurization became standard in the wine-making industry and was adopted by vintners throughout France. It wasn't long before the wine-making industries of other countries followed suit. Eventually other industries, such as the dairy industry and the beer-making industry, adopted the pasteurization process and continue to use it to this day.

PASTEUR TURNS TO MEDICINE

By 1871, Pasteur's work with silkworms was completed. He had also finished his work on the spoilage of wine. His stroke a few years earlier had slowed him down physically. But his mind was as sharp as ever, and he had lost none of his arrogant confidence. He was ready for a new challenge.

For several years he had thought about studying human diseases. All of his scientific work, from his first experiments with crystals to the conclusions about silkworm diseases, had made him question accepted

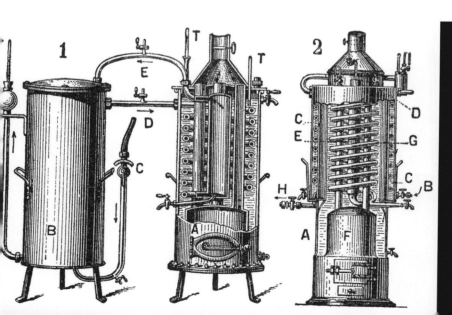

This illustration shows the various parts of early Pasteurization equipment.

medical wisdom. He began to realize that his discoveries might be applied to human diseases.

There were a few problems, however. First, he wasn't a doctor or a medical scientist. He was a chemist. In the 1800s, the scientific community believed that chemistry had little to do with medicine or biology. Pasteur knew that the medical community would not consider a chemist, not even a celebrated chemist like Pasteur, to be qualified to study human disease. Second, he was still a professor with the French education system. How would he have the time to devote to new studies?

Pasteur found the solution by resigning from the École Normale Supérieure in 1872, citing his ill health as a result of his stroke as the reason. He requested that he be allowed to continue as the director of his new laboratory, which had been constructed for him during his illness. As director he would continue to receive a salary, but he would be relieved of all academic duties. His request was granted. Pasteur was fifty years old, an age at which most scientists were long past their discovery days. But

The Four Humors

During the Middle Ages the theory of "humors" as a cause of disease became accepted. This theory stated that the body contained four main fluids, or humors. These humors were yellow bile, black bile, phlegm and blood. If one of these components was out of proportion in the body, disease occurred. The imbalance was called isonomia.

Pasteur was about to launch one of the most remarkable phases of his career, one that revolutionized medicine.

WHAT CAUSES HUMAN DISEASE?

Humankind had been aware of the terrible effects of sickness and disease since its emergence. But no one had any idea how and why disease occurred. People living in ancient civilizations believed that disease was brought on by the gods or by other magical occurrences. Some believed that disease was a form of punishment for wrongdoing. When deadly epidemics swept through a city, they might be blamed on the air, the soil, or the water.

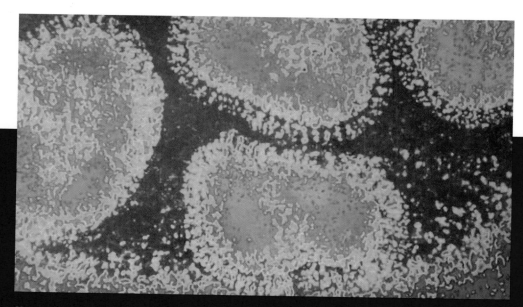

Under the microscope, this is what the influenza (flu) virus looks like

Scientists and physicians began to suspect that diseases were transmitted from one person to another through physical contact. Some even put forth the idea that tiny living beings caused disease when they were taken into the body by breathing contaminated air or eating contaminated food. This theory was discounted most of the time because there was no way to prove it.

When the microscope was invented, scientists could see bacteria and other microorganisms for the first time. Once again many scientists suspected that they were somehow the cause of disease. Others scoffed at the idea. They couldn't believe that something so tiny could cause such terrible sickness.

By the 1800s, there were great arguments raging in the scientific community, but everyone agreed that medicine did not do much to help the people suffering from diseases. Hundreds of remedies existed for every type of sickness. Some worked, some didn't, and no one was quite sure why.

Pasteur was one of the scientists who strongly believed in the theory that living organisms caused disease. He had formed these ideas through his experiments and conclusions with fermentation, spontaneous generation, and silkworm diseases. He also read about the ideas and experiments of other scientists who believed in this theory. Although the ideas he embraced were not new, Pasteur was the first scientist to put them all together to form a coherent germ theory of disease. This included how sickness began, was transmitted, and—most importantly—how it could be treated and prevented. It was this leap of brilliance—combining everything he knew into one overarching idea—that made Pasteur's work great.

PASTEUR DIVES INTO MEDICINE

The first thing Pasteur needed to do was join the medical community. If he could do this, his ideas would be more respected. In 1873, he became a member of the Academy of Medicine, an organization similar to the Academy of Sciences, but which consisted of physicians, surgeons, and pharmacists.

When Pasteur joined this organization, he was already completely convinced that microorganisms, or germs, were the cause of disease. He was equally convinced that many diseases and sicknesses were transmitted through carelessness, dirt, and ignorance. With his usual flair and self-assuredness, Pasteur set out to convince the medical community of his ideas.

Pasteur visited hospitals and consulted with physicians. He was horrified at the conditions he saw in the hospital wards. Patients were lined up in rows of narrow beds, with only curtains separating them. Wound dressings went unchanged, sheets remained soiled, and pans of human waste and pus- and blood-soaked bandages sat under the beds. Visitors, doctors, nurses, and patients came and went constantly, creating a steady buzz of noise and movement. Pasteur knew that these crowded hospitals were infested with germs, and it was these germs that caused infection and death. He just had to figure out a way to prove it.

With his usual thoroughness, Pasteur began by treating surgical patients, dressing their wounds with antiseptic solutions and cotton-wool bandages. The antiseptic killed germs, and the bandages prevented new germs from infecting the wounds. Pasteur saw results immediately. The bandaged wounds healed, and the patients did not get sicker because of infections, which was common at the time. He had shown that when germs are blocked from getting into a wound, the wound heals.

Pasteur began to think of other ways to block germs from invading the body. One way, he theorized, was to kill the germs *before* they came into contact with a wound. It was at about this time that the world heard this from another scientist.

JOSEPH LISTER AND ANTISEPSIS

A bright Scottish scientist named Joseph Lister had read Pasteur's paper on fermentation and became convinced that there was a connection

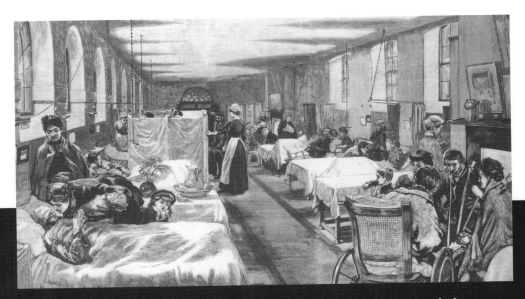

After Pasteur joined the Academy of Medicine, he visited many crowded hospitals. He believed that these dirty conditions allowed germs to spread infection and cause death.

between decaying organic matter and disease. He theorized that most germs were airborne, so he developed a special antiseptic solution, carbolic acid, that was to be sprayed into the air before surgeries and other medical procedures.

Most physicians ignored Lister's ideas. Even the ones who thought he was onto something didn't like the idea of methodically spraying

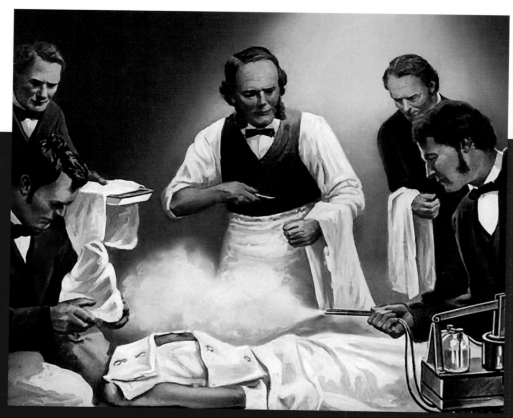

Joseph Lister developed a special antiseptic spray of carbolic acid to be used before surgeries and other medical procedures.

"Mankind Is Being Benefited by Your Labors"

In 1874, Joseph Lister wrote a letter to the world-renowned Pasteur. In it, he thanked Pasteur for inspiring him to a new understanding of disease, "Allow me to take this opportunity to tender you my most cordial thanks for having, by your brilliant researches, demonstrated to me the truth of the germ theory . . . and thus furnished me with the principle upon which alone the antiseptic system can be carried out. Should you at any time visit Edinburgh it would, I believe, give you sincere gratification to see at our hospital how largely mankind is being benefited by your labors."

everything with carbolic acid before operating on patients. A few, however, did believe in Lister's ideas. The physicians and surgeons who adopted Lister's idea of cleanliness and antiseptic use began to see fewer infections and better survival rates in their patients than other doctors.

Pasteur and Lister began communicating in 1874, and Lister told Pasteur about his successes with carbolic acid. Pasteur immediately understood that Lister was correct, and he embraced Lister's ideas. Pasteur took Lister's ideas farther. He, along with other scientists, realized that germs were transmitted not only through the air, but through contaminated hands, sponges, instruments, and other objects. Pasteur began to advise French physicians to clean wounds with antiseptic solutions and to sterilize their bandages and instruments as well.

THE MEDICAL FIELD IS SLOW TO ADOPT PASTEUR'S IDEAS

Even though Pasteur proved over and over that his ideas about cleanliness and germs were correct, the vast majority of physicians refused to listen. All that washing and cleaning was useless, they insisted, because germs did not cause diseases. Pasteur's ideas were in direct conflict with centuries-old theories and traditions of medicine. At the time, surgical procedures were done in small, close rooms crowded with students and observers, all in their regular clothing, sitting on ordinary furniture that may or may not be clean. Sometimes surgeons would walk from room to room, operating on more than one patient at a time and using the same instruments for all of them. Many surgeons proudly wore the same

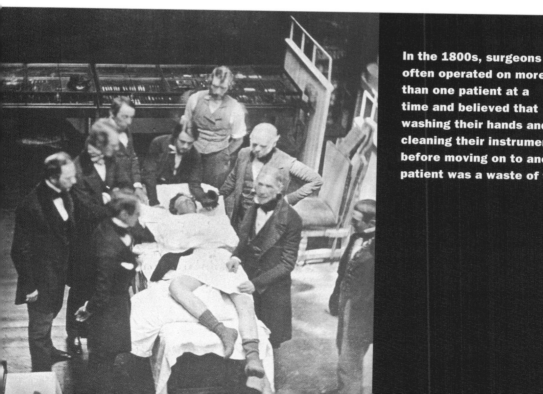

In the 1800s, surgeons often operated on more than one patient at a time and believed that washing their hands and cleaning their instruments before moving on to another patient was a waste of time.

blood-stained clothing and aprons as a symbol of how good they were as doctors. They didn't want to change these ways, and they resented a mere chemist for suggesting they should.

Pasteur's ideas could not be ignored for long, however. Doctors began to try Pasteur's antiseptic procedures. Immediately, the mortality rate for surgery plummeted. Slowly, more doctors adopted the procedures that Pasteur so strongly fought for—cleaning instruments, using only sterile bandages, washing hands before touching patients, wearing clean clothing—and realized he was right. The germ theory of disease was correct, and Pasteur had proved it.

Eventually the entire medical community embraced the ideas of antiseptic cleanliness. The procedures Pasteur advocated became, and still are, standard in every doctor's office and hospital in the world.

Pasteur Speaks Out

Pasteur impressed on his physician colleagues that avoidance of microbes meant avoidance of infection. In a famous speech delivered to the Academy of Medicine in Paris, he stated, "This water, this sponge, this lint with which you wash or cover a wound, may deposit germs which have the power of multiplying rapidly within the tissue. . . . If I had the honor of being a surgeon . . . not only would I use none but perfectly clean instruments, but I would clean my hands with the greatest care. . . . I would use only lint, bandages and sponges previously exposed to a temperature of 1300 to 1500 degrees." Slowly but surely, through the preaching of Pasteur, Lister, and other physicians, antiseptic medicine and surgery became the rule.

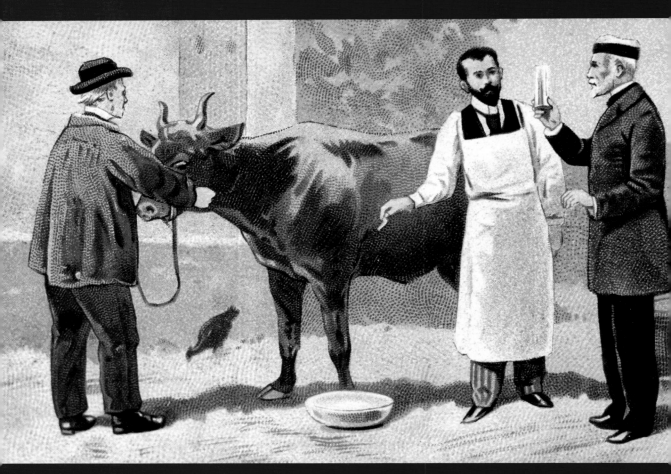

This postcard depicts Pasteur's work with agriculture. Thousands of animals died each year from anthrax.

CHAPTER NINE

Pasteur and Anthrax

*I*n 1877, Pasteur was fifty-five years old and counted among the greatest scientists in France and perhaps the world. He had achieved all that he had set out to do as a young, brash science student in the 1840s. He had made discoveries that revolutionized science.

He had proven that microbes traveled through the air and through the intestinal tracts of silkworms. He had shown that spontaneous generation was false. He knew that good hygiene could prevent diseases in silkworms. His discoveries with pasteurization had shown that heat could kill harmful bacteria. He had shown that hygiene and cleanliness could stop the spread of harmful germs that caused sickness and disease. He single-handedly invented the science of microbiology and had proven that the germ theory of disease was correct.

A Disease Slips by Pasteur

Pasteur had opportunities to study diseases in humans before 1877. In the later part of 1865, the French government had asked a team of scientists to investigate a terrible outbreak of cholera. At the time, cholera was a deadly disease that claimed thousands of lives each year, and no one knew how it was transmitted.

The scientists set to work. Pasteur and the others were convinced that a specific germ caused the disease, but they had to find it. They theorized that the germ was airborne, so they tested the air, took samples of dust, and even shook out the sheets and clothing of victims and filled flasks with air. They took blood samples and examined the patients. But in the end they did not find the germ or figure out how it was transmitted. Pasteur and the team failed.

What Pasteur and the other scientists didn't know at the time was that the cholera bacterium was not transmitted through the air. Instead, the bacterium is transmitted by contaminated food or drinking water. It would take several more years of study and experimentation for researchers to determine this.

By this time, he had completely turned away from chemistry and was focused on medicine. Most of his work with germs and diseases had been done through observation, study, and theory. Now, Pasteur felt it was time for him to dig deeper into the mysteries of human disease. He wanted to discover the exact role of the germ: how it worked and why it caused disease.

PASTEUR FIGHTS ANTHRAX

In early 1877, Pasteur was contacted by France's minister of agriculture. Pasteur's success with the silkworm problem had prompted the minister to contact him regarding a new concern. Anthrax was a continuing problem with French agriculture. Thousands of animals died each year, which hurt farming industries. Pasteur was asked whether he could do anything to help the farmers of France combat this terrible disease. Pasteur hesitated; this would take him away from studying infectious diseases in humans. Once again, he felt the lure of a challenge, so he agreed.

ANTHRAX: THE TERRIBLE DISEASE

In the 1800s, anthrax was one of the most dreaded diseases to strike domestic animals. Other countries in Europe also faced this disease, which struck horses, oxen, cows, and sheep. Hundreds of thousands of

In 1865, Pasteur and a team of scientists were asked to study the disease cholera. The scientists believed it was one germ that caused the disease that claimed thousands of lives.

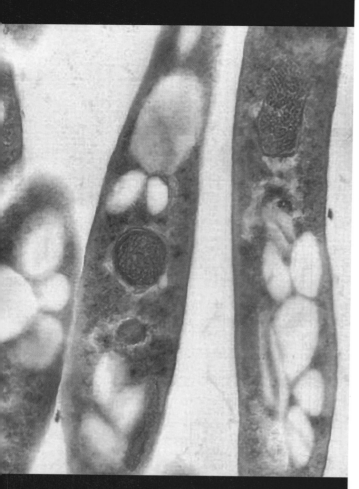

This rod-shaped bacteria is anthrax. By studying the bacteria, Pasteur was able to conclude that different bacteria caused different diseases.

animals around the world died. The worst part was that the disease seemed to strike without warning, causing healthy animals to drop dead in a few hours.

No one knew how the disease was caused or spread. Farmers did realize that pastures became poisoned after an outbreak of anthrax. Sometimes a human who had come into contact with a dead or dying animal was also struck down. A few scientists had suggested that the disease was caused by toxic plants or herbs, but no one had found the real cause.

OTHER SCIENTISTS PAVE THE WAY FOR PASTEUR

A few scientists around the world had already made several discoveries about anthrax before Pasteur approached the problem. Casimir-Joseph Davaine, a fellow French scientist, had been the first person to identify the rod-shaped anthrax bacteria in the 1850s. At the time, however, he was unsure whether this bacteria was the cause of the disease or something that occurred as a result of the infection.

In the 1870s, a German scientist named Robert Koch saw the rod-shaped anthrax bacteria when he looked at animal blood under a microscope. He took his experiments further, however, by growing the anthrax bacteria and reproducing the disease in animal tissue that had not been infected. Koch was very close to finding the answer to how the bacteria was transmitted, but other scientists refuted Koch's theories. This was when Pasteur joined the fray.

DEAD ANIMALS EVERYWHERE

Pasteur was convinced that Koch was correct, but he had to prove it. He first had to prove that it was indeed the rod-shaped bacteria that caused anthrax. He put a drop of infected blood into a flask of urine, which is a good medium for growing bacteria. After a few days, Pasteur put a drop of that liquid into a flask of fresh urine. He repeated this experiment over and over, diluting the original drop of blood until all that he had left was urine and the anthrax bacteria. The next step was to prove that the bacteria were still alive. He injected some of the urine into a rabbit, which immediately died.

Pasteur's next experiments consisted of examining the bodies of animals that had died of anthrax at different times. He discovered that the longer a dead body was left on the ground to rot, the more disease-making bacteria, including anthrax, could be found in it. When he isolated the different bacteria, he discovered that they caused different illnesses. Pasteur proved that not only did bacteria cause disease but that different bacteria caused different diseases. Even then, the scientific community was unconvinced.

PASTEUR AND THE CHICKENS

One of Pasteur's most vocal critics was a professor of veterinary medicine named Gabriel Colin. He didn't believe any of Pasteur's conclusions. The

Pasteur found that chickens did not die of anthrax because their body temperatures were too high.

two quarreled for months. Scientists at the Academy of Medicine began to take sides. At one point, Pasteur noted that chickens did not catch anthrax. Colin insisted that they did. Pasteur offered to prove that they did not. Colin agreed. Pasteur sent Colin a broth full of anthrax bacteria and asked Colin to inject it into healthy chickens. Sure that Pasteur was wrong, Colin gleefully did so.

A week later Pasteur saw Colin and asked him, "How are my chickens doing?" Colin had to admit that they weren't dead yet. A few weeks later the men met again, and Pasteur asked the same question. Soon, Colin insisted, they would be dead. Months later Colin had to admit defeat. The chickens did not die of anthrax.

Pasteur triumphantly stated, "Now I will prove that chickens can die of anthrax!" He theorized that the chickens had not died because their body temperature was too high. The high temperature, he believed, killed the anthrax bacteria. To prove this, he took several chickens and plunged them into a cold bath, then injected them with anthrax. The chickens died. Scientists found anthrax bacteria swimming in their blood. Pasteur had proven that outside factors such as temperature could affect the transmission of disease. This was an enormous discovery that would have far-reaching effects on the study of medicine.

Pasteur wasn't finished with anthrax yet. He then had to find out how the disease was transmitted. To do this he took field trips all over France, studying fields that had been used by animals with anthrax. He thought the disease might be spread by contaminated food, so he fed lab animals anthrax-poisoned grasses and vegetation. In many cases the animals didn't die. Then he noticed that animals that ate tough, sharp grasses died in greater numbers than animals that had been fed softer grasses.

After many experiments he realized that the sharp grasses cut the mouths of the animals, allowing the anthrax bacteria to enter the body through the wounds. This led him to conclude that anthrax bacteria had infected the pastures themselves.

A CLUE IN THE FIELDS

One more thing bothered Pasteur. How did the bacteria climb all the way through the soil, from the buried animals, to contaminate the grass and animals far above?

Pasteur hit upon the answer as he walked through a field one day. He noticed that in one part of the field, the soil was darker than the surrounding soil. The farmer told him that it was the spot where he had buried several animals that had died of anthrax. When Pasteur examined the soil closely, he saw the tunnels and mounds of earth made by earthworms as they dug through the soil. The earthworms carried the anthrax from the dead animals, through the earth and brought it to the surface. Pasteur discovered anthrax bacteria in the intestinal tracts of the earthworms. The worms carried the bacteria but did not contract the disease. When they ingested the earth, and then expelled it, the dirt became contaminated.

Pasteur urged farmers to prevent their animals from grazing in fields where dead bodies were buried. He suggested that farmers bury dead animals in sandy soil or other places where earthworms couldn't live. These simple measures transformed the farming industry and virtually eliminated anthrax from French agriculture. Anthrax did continue to kill animals, but not on the huge scale it once had.

Through Pasteur's anthrax experimentation, he had made a series of profound discoveries about disease and its transmission. He showed that disease was affected by temperature and by the way a body ingested bacteria. He proved that bacteria could affect different organisms differently, or not at all. He showed that bacteria can be carried by animals that do not get the disease, in the case of the earthworms. In the next few years, he and the rest of the medical world would build on these revolutionary discoveries.

Farmers began burning the bodies of animals that died of anthrax when it was discovered that anthrax could spread through earthworms.

Le Petit Journal

TOUS LES JOURS
Le Petit Journal
5 Centimes

SUPPLÉMENT ILLUSTRÉ
Huit pages : CINQ centimes

TOUS LES VENDREDIS
Le Supplément illustré
5 Centimes

Quatrième Année — SAMEDI 14 JANVIER 1893 — Numéro 112

LE JUBILÉ DE M. PASTEUR
A la Sorbonne

Pasteur was honored for his many accomplishments in medicine at a Jubilee at the Sorbonne in Paris. He had become of one the most famous scientists in the world.

CHAPTER TEN

Father of Immunology

*A*lthough Pasteur was not a doctor, he became passionate about preventing human diseases. His work until that point suggested that there might be some way to prevent terrible diseases in humans.

Most scientists and physicians at the time realized that individuals who had once caught certain diseases became resistant to those diseases. No one really understood why or how this happened. Science had yet to discover the secrets of the human immune system. Science was, however, aware of the concept of inoculation, which had been somewhat successful in preventing certain diseases. Pasteur had heard of several other scientists who had experimented with inoculation to stop disease, most notably the English physician Edward Jenner.

JENNER: A COUNTRY DOCTOR DEFEATS SMALLPOX

In the late 1790s, an outbreak of smallpox hit rural areas of England. Edward Jenner, a country doctor in Gloucestershire, England, was aware of the belief among dairy workers that if a milker had contracted cowpox (a mild disease similar to smallpox), he or she was immune to smallpox. Jenner speculated that purposefully infecting a person with cowpox would protect him or her from the much more severe smallpox.

In 1798, Jenner inoculated (introduced into) a young boy, James Phipps, with fluid obtained from a blister on the hand of a milkmaid infected with cowpox. The boy became sick with cowpox, but recovered in a few days. Several weeks later Jenner inoculated the boy with smallpox. He did not contract the disease. Jenner had successfully inoculated a human being against a deadly disease. He called these inoculations vaccines, from the Latin word vacca, which means "cow."

Jenner made his discovery almost one hundred years before Pasteur began his experiments with inoculations. In that time, the medical community first rejected then accepted Jenner's ideas. Although inoculation was known and used in Pasteur's time, no one really understood how it worked. There was still a great deal of fear and confusion about the procedure, and the scientific community was still deeply divided about performing it.

Jenner had unlocked a door that Pasteur would throw wide open. Pasteur wanted to figure out how to create artificial cultures of all known diseases and to find out how to vaccinate against them all. At the age of sixty, the self-confident Pasteur was convinced he could do it.

MORE SICK CHICKENS FOR PASTEUR

Pasteur's first experiments were with the disease chicken cholera. It was known that chicken cholera, which is not related to human cholera, was caused by a specific bacteria. Pasteur began by cultivating the bacteria in his lab. Over the months, he collected dozens of flasks filled with the chicken cholera bacteria.

What happened next is legendary. When Pasteur left for vacation that summer, he accidentally left a flask of the bacteria behind in the lab. Weeks later when Pasteur returned, he resumed his experiments and began injecting chickens with different experimental cultures, including the one he had left on the shelf for so long. He was shocked when eight chickens injected with the old culture did not get sick or die.

At first he was upset, because he had believed the old culture was still as strong as the new ones. He prepared a fresh batch of bacteria and injected the eight chickens, plus several others. The newly injected chickens died, but the eight chickens injected with the old culture remained healthy. Pasteur tried several more times to infect these chickens, but they refused to die. He realized that the original eight chickens that had been injected with the old culture were no longer susceptible to the disease.

Pasteur was confused by this conclusion. He and other scientists had assumed that bacteria would always remain at full strength and cause disease. What this discovery showed was that bacteria could be weakened. He also realized that outside forces could cause it to weaken. Pasteur called these inoculations with weakened bacteria vaccines, out of respect to Jenner, who had coined the term years before.

Finally, through experimentation, he came to the conclusion that the same bacteria could have different strengths and cause diseases to be more or less severe. He also realized that an animal that was exposed to a weaker version of a bacteria could become immune to the disease it caused without becoming sick.

Pasteur began using this idea to develop a new vaccine. Anthrax was still fresh in his mind, so he chose to work with that disease. Soon Pasteur had developed a weaker version of the anthrax bacteria in his lab. He was sure that vaccinating animals with this weaker version would make them immune to the disease.

When Pasteur announced his conclusions, they threw the medical world into chaos. Scientists attacked him at every turn, including many in the academy. A medical journal of the time described the outpouring of opposition, saying that instead of receiving the attention and admiration that he deserved, Pasteur encountered frantic opposition from people who barely listened to him, and wanted to tear him down. Many of these were doctors who openly criticized Pasteur because he was not a doctor himself.

Outwardly, Pasteur was defiant and confident, but he grew sad and weary from all the attacks, confiding in his closest friends how upset they made him. In typical form, Pasteur did not back down. He knew he was right, and he also knew he could prove it. He offered to demonstrate his conclusions. He would inoculate a set of sheep with the anthrax vaccine then later inject them with the bacteria. If Pasteur was right, the vaccinated sheep would not die of the disease. Few believed he could do it.

THE SHEEP OF POUILLY-LE-FORT

May 5, 1881, was a beautiful day. Pasteur had found a farmer in the French countryside who agreed to provide animals for Pasteur's demonstration. The farm was crowded with scientists, administrators, reporters, doctors, veterinarians, and the public. The now-famous Dr. Lister was among them. The atmosphere was like that of a country fair. Some people supported Pasteur. Many of them, however, had come to see Pasteur fail.

Pasteur and his assistants vaccinated twenty-four sheep, one goat, and six cows with five drops of the living, yet weakened, anthrax bacteria. Three weeks later Pasteur and his assistants returned to the farm and gave them a second vaccination of the weakened anthrax bacteria. Then, on May 31, all of the animals, along with twenty-five more sheep and three cows, received an injection of full-strength anthrax bacteria. Pasteur predicted that the second group of animals would die within two days, while the inoculated group would survive.

Pasteur used sheep to demonstrate the anthrax vaccination. The vaccination consisted of three separate injections.

Everyone anxiously watched the animals. By June 2, 1881, all of the non-vaccinated animals had died. One of the vaccinated animals died, but it was later discovered that it died of pregnancy complications, not anthrax.

INTERNATIONAL FAME

Papers all over France proclaimed Pasteur's victory. Even foreign papers, such as the London *Times,* carried news of Pasteur's stunning success with the vaccine. The scientific community could no longer fight Pasteur's ideas in the face of such evidence.

The French government honored Pasteur with the Legion of

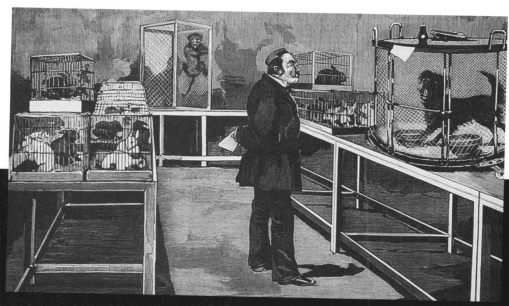

Pasteur worked to create a vaccination for rabies. At the time, rabies in humans was a rare but deadly disease.

Honor, an award given for significant contributions that enhanced France's international reputation. Requests for the vaccine, and for Pasteur, poured in from around the world. He attended banquets and parties in his honor. Entire towns and city governments came to greet him upon his arrival in new places. Pasteur had become one of the world's most famous scientists.

The results of Pasteur's triumph were seen in the French agricultural industry almost immediately. Within ten years more than three million sheep and half a million cattle had been vaccinated. The death rate from anthrax was reduced to less than 1 percent.

Pasteur, flushed with the successes of his work with chicken cholera and anthrax, began to work with other bacteria and diseases. Over the next few years, he isolated the microbes that caused several diseases, including childbirth fever and pneumonia.

PASTEUR DEFEATS RABIES

Pasteur's successes with the anthrax vaccine only spurred him to work harder to defeat other diseases. He had figured out how to prevent an animal disease through vaccination, but that wasn't enough. Now, he wondered, could vaccinations be used to cure human diseases? Pasteur believed they could. At the same time he and his coworkers were defeating anthrax, they were working with dogs in an attempt to prevent rabies. At the time, rabies was a rare but deadly disease, transmitted to humans through the bite of an infected animal. People and animals who contracted rabies suffered terribly for weeks then died agonizing deaths. Because of this rabies was a feared and hated disease.

STRICT EXPERIMENTS, STRANGE RESULTS

Pasteur knew that the disease was transmitted through saliva. He and his partner, Émile Roux, a physician who had been Pasteur's assistant and collaborator for several years, tried to infect healthy dogs by injecting them with the saliva of rabid animals. To their surprise, this didn't always work. Through more experimentation, they discovered that the active rabies microorganisms were located in a diseased animal's brain and spinal cord.

With this information Pasteur was soon able to transfer rabies from diseased animals and consistently reproduce the sickness in healthy animals by placing spinal cord tissue from rabid animals in contact with the brains of healthy animals.

Why Rabies?

Of all the diseases Pasteur could have tried to cure, why did he choose a relatively rare one such as rabies? The answer might lie in Pasteur's childhood. Stories say that when Pasteur was a boy, he heard of a rabid wolf that roamed through the Arbois region where he lived. People in his village were bitten by this diseased animal and died terrible deaths. Pasteur is said to have remembered the fear that swept through his town, and it was this memory that made him decide to tackle rabies. At the same time, Pasteur was always interested in publicizing his research. He undoubtedly considered that a cure for rabies would further increase his international fame.

The next step was to develop a vaccine that would provide protection to a person or animal that had already contracted the disease. Pasteur and Roux experimented with vaccines containing microorganisms that were decreased in strength by having undergone several days of aging. They finally hit upon the right number of vaccinations, in the right strengths, that would prevent a dog from getting sick from rabies, even after being infected. The only way they could know for sure if their vaccine would work in humans would be to test it on humans. Roux and Pasteur believed that more experiments were required before they could test their product on humans.

JOSEPH MEISTER COMES TO PASTEUR

In July 1885, a nine-year-old named Joseph Meister was bitten by a rabid dog. His parents knew that he would certainly die, and they traveled from

Pasteur cured nine-year-old Joseph Meister of rabies by giving him a vaccination that had only been given to animals.

Joseph Meister

After Pasteur cured the young Joseph Meister, they remained friends, writing one another letters and staying in contact as Meister grew up. Later, Meister would be hired by the Pasteur Institute as a guard and gatekeeper. In the 1940s, during World War II, the Germans who were occupying Paris came to the Institute to see the tomb of the great Pasteur, but they were blocked by Meister, who guarded the tomb entrance.

their rural home to Paris, desperately hoping that Pasteur could help them.

Pasteur was hesitant to try the vaccine on the boy, but everyone knew the boy would certainly die if something wasn't done to help him. Pasteur gave Joseph his vaccinations. After receiving the vaccine, Joseph survived. His parents and Pasteur were overjoyed. Joseph was the first person to survive rabies by being given Pasteur's vaccinations.

Pasteur's new discoveries became known throughout the world in a matter of weeks. People flocked to Pasteur's lab in Paris, begging for help. He could not refuse, so he agreed to set up a center for the treatment of rabies in his laboratory. By the end of 1885, only six months after Joseph Meister was cured, eighty treatments had been performed. For years, this antirabies treatment would be known as "the Pasteur treatment."

THE PASTEUR INSTITUTE

Pasteur was sixty-three years old when he triumphed over rabies. Although he was elated by his success, he was also worn out from his years of hard work and from defending himself against the relentless criticisms he'd faced throughout his career. He was growing physically weak, as he had never fully regained his strength after his stroke twenty years earlier. He was ready to step away from active research.

At the same time, the little clinic he had opened up in his laboratory was growing. People from around the world flocked to the small lab, hoping for a cure for rabies. As patients arrived, there arose a need for other services, such as medical examinations, first aid, vaccinations, paperwork, and other duties. There were no waiting rooms or examination areas. People lined up through the lab, waiting for their shots. The clinic was overwhelmed.

Pasteur began to think of creating a clinic that could provide medical treatment for more people. He envisioned that this medical clinic would not be sponsored by a university or the government. Instead, it would be funded through private donations, gifts, and subscriptions. This way, the clinic would be free to pursue any research it felt was necessary.

Several wealthy Frenchmen were excited by the idea and offered money. A subscription drive was established that raised millions of francs for the new clinic. Pasteur's colleagues found an area outside Paris that was perfect for the new clinic.

On November 14, 1888, the Pasteur Institute was opened. Although the institute was begun as a center for delivering rabies vaccinations, Pasteur knew that it would become much more. He envisioned the institute as a top-rate medical facility that would study and investigate contagious diseases and microbes. The institute would become one of the foremost medical institutions in the world.

On November 14, 1888, the Pasteur Institute opened providing vaccinations, medical examinations, and research.

Pasteur, now sixty-six years old and becoming frail, arrived at the dedication of the institute supported by his son, Jean-Baptiste. The crowd was filled with scientists from around the world, many of whom had fought with Pasteur over the years. They all waited for Pasteur to give a speech. Instead, his son read his words for him. What no one knew was that a year before Pasteur had suffered a series of strokes that made it difficult for him to speak. Rather than being embarrassed by his voice, Pasteur chose not to speak at all.

A TRIUMPH OF SCIENCE

By this time, Pasteur rarely left his home in Paris. Each day Marie read the newspapers to him to save his failing eyesight. He still traveled to the institute and continued to keep up with the new facility and its work. The scientists who had begun working at the institute visited him frequently, keeping him informed of the experiments and seeking his advice on scientific questions.

The institute became everything Pasteur hoped it would be. The best scientists in the world clamored to be accepted to the institute as research scientists. One of its goals was to train scientists, and the best and brightest students from around the world went there to study. They studied scientific fields that, until Pasteur's work, had not existed, such as microbiology and immunology.

The scientists at the institute believed passionately, as Pasteur himself did, that healing sickness included having knowledge of many things, such as science, medicine, hygiene, and disease prevention. Health and education went together. Science could benefit humankind through its applications to industry and to the health field. These ideas, first known as the Pasteurian approach, eventually gained acceptance around the world. Today, these concepts are common in medicine and science, but it was one man, Louis Pasteur, who gave them to the world.

A QUIET END

For the last few years of his life, Pasteur ventured out less and less frequently. Occasionally he visited the institute, but most of the time he remained in his home with Marie, who remained devoted to her husband. On November 1, 1894, Pasteur fainted and collapsed. He remained bedridden for three months. His family, including his two surviving children, Jean-Baptiste and Marie-Louise, and their families, moved to be closer to Pasteur. His recovery was slow, but, by the spring of 1895, Pasteur had recovered enough to once again make rare trips outside his home.

He was on his way home from a visit to the institute in June 1895 when he became weak. He soon became bedridden once again. This time there would be no recovery. His family and friends stayed by his side, reading to him and recounting the events of the day, scientific discussions, and political happenings. In September, Pasteur had yet another stroke, and on September 28, 1895, Pasteur died quietly in his home, surrounded by the people he loved.

The French government immediately ordered a state funeral. Thousands of people lined the streets and followed the hearse as it made its way slowly through the Parisian streets. According to his wishes, Pasteur was buried in a tomb built for him in the cellars of the institute. He remains there today, watching over the institute he founded.

PASTEUR'S LEGACY

It is difficult to list all of Pasteur's achievements and the ways that they affected the world, for there are so many. Pasteur was the first scientist to become deeply involved in experimental medicine. He was among the first to understand the importance of science to the world and to apply it to industries such as agriculture and medicine. He was one of the few scientists who saw the connections between biology, chemistry, medicine, and health and worked all his life to use his ideas to benefit humankind. He invented pasteurization and revolutionized the idea of vaccinations. He created entirely new areas of scientific study, including microbiology and immunology.

Almost everything that is a part of everyday life today has been affected or transformed by Pasteur and his ideas. From washing hands before eating a meal to disinfecting city sewage drains, from childhood immunizations to the latest research on AIDS and other diseases, from health and safety regulations in industry to the pasteurized milk in the refrigerator, every person in the world has benefited from Pasteur and his work.

Pasteur was a pioneer in the medical field. Because of his research and discovery of vaccinations, he was able to educate many. He is pictured here with children bitten by rabid dogs.

Timeline

LOUIS PASTEUR'S LIFE	WORLD EVENTS

1822 Louis Pasteur is born on December 27 in Dole, France.

1827 The Pasteur family moves to Arbois.

1837 Victoria becomes queen of England.

1838 Pasteur and friend Jules Vercel leave for Paris. Pasteur returns home a month later.

1840 Pasteur graduates from the college at Besançon. He becomes a teaching assistant.

1841 Pasteur fails the exam for his bachelor of science degree.

1842 Pasteur retakes and passes the exam and is awarded a bachelor of science degree.

1844 Pasteur enters the École Normale Supérieure.

1845 Pasteur graduates from the École Normale Supérieure.

1848 Pasteur is appointed professor of chemistry at Strasbourg University.

1849 Pasteur marries Marie Laurent.

1850 Pasteur's daughter Jeanne is born on April 2.

1851 Pasteur's son Jean-Baptiste is born on November 8.

1853 Pasteur's daughter Cécile is born on October 1.

1854 Pasteur begins his job as professor of chemistry and dean of the Faculty of Sciences at the University of Lille.

1857 Pasteur publishes a paper on lactic fermentation.

1858 Pasteur's daughter Marie-Louise is born on July 19.

1859 Pasteur's daughter Jeanne dies at Arbois of typhoid fever.

Charles Darwin publishes *On the Origin of Species.*

1860 Pasteur publishes a paper on alcoholic fermentation.

1861 The American Civil War begins.

1862 Pasteur is elected to the Academy of Sciences.

1863 Pasteur begins to study wine spoilage. His daughter Camille is born on July 24. He becomes a professor at the École Normale Supérieure.

1865 Pasteur's father, Jean-Joseph dies on June 15, and his daughter Camille dies on September 11. He begins his silkworm research.

1865 The American Civil War ends.

1866 Pasteur's daughter Cecile dies on May 23.

1868 Pasteur suffers a stroke.

1872 Pasteur retires, citing health issues. He is elected to the Academy of Medicine.

1873 Pasteur develops the germ theory of disease.

Europe experiences an economic crisis.

1877 Pasteur begins his research on anthrax.

1879 Thomas Alva Edison invents the electric light.

1881 Pasteur conducts a successful anthrax vaccination experiment at Pouilly-le-Fort.

1884 Pasteur begins his work on rabies.

1885 Nine-year-old Joseph Meister is vaccinated against rabies and survives.

1888 The Pasteur Institute opens.

1894 Pasteur dies on September 28.

To Find Out More

BOOKS

Ackerman, Jane. *Louis Pasteur and the Founding of Microbiology.* Greensboro, N.C.: Morgan Reynolds Publishing, 2004.

Alphin, Elaine Marie. *Germ Hunter: A Story about Louis Pasteur.* Minneapolis: Carolrhoda Books, 2003.

Birch, Beverly. *Louis Pasteur: Father of Modern Medicine.* San Diego: Blackbirch Press, 2001.

Robbins, Louise. *Louis Pasteur and the Hidden World of Microbes.* New York: Oxford University Press, 2001.

Smith, Linda Wasmer. *Louis Pasteur: Disease Fighter.* New Jersey: Enslow Publishers, 2001.

ORGANIZATIONS AND ONLINE SITES

Founders of Science
http://www.foundersofscience.net

This site is devoted to Pasteur and other experts in the fields of biological and medical sciences.

Pasteur Institute
25-28 rue du Dr Roux
75015 Paris FRANCE

The facility that Pasteur founded continues to be one of the world's most respected institutions of medical research.

Pasteur Institute at Lille
1, rue du Professor Calmette
BP 245
59019 LILLE Cedex FRANCE

More than six hundred doctors and scientists conduct research projects at this facility.

Pasteur Museum
http://www.pasteur.fr/pasteur/musees/museesUS/index.htm

Pasteur's private apartment at the Pasteur Institute is now home to this museum, which is dedicated to the memory of the scientist's life and work.

A Note on Sources

Until the 1990s, the standard biography of Pasteur was *The Life of Pasteur,* written by his son-in-law Rene Vallery-Radot. In 1995, two new biographies of Pasteur were published, both to commemorate the one hundredth anniversary of his death. The two works, both comprehensive, take radically different views of the great scientist. *Louis Pasteur* by Patrice Debre is an exhaustive and detailed look at not only Pasteur's public scientific achievements, but also at his intimate life and relationships with his father, family, and friends. *The Private Life of Louis Pasteur* by Gerald Geison, on the other hand, is to call into question some of Pasteur's most famous discoveries, not their accuracy or Pasteur's achievements, but rather the scientific methods he used to come to the conclusions he did. All three of these books have become standard sources of information about the legendary scientist, and each give a different perspective of Pasteur's life and work.

—*Allison Lassieur*

Index

About the Author

Allison Lassieur has written more than fifty books about famous figures, history, world cultures, current events, and science. In addition to writing, Lassieur studies medieval textile history. She lives in Pennsylvania in a one-hundred-year-old house with her husband, Charles.